AMERICAN VISTAS
1607–1877

American Vistas
1607-1877

Edited by **LEONARD DINNERSTEIN**
UNIVERSITY OF ARIZONA

AND **KENNETH T. JACKSON**
COLUMBIA UNIVERSITY

New York **OXFORD UNIVERSITY PRESS**
London 1971 Toronto

For
Barbara Jackson
and
Myra Dinnerstein

PREFACE

Perhaps more than any other generation in American history, college students of the 1970's have grown up in an age of almost constant domestic and international crisis. Aware of and extremely concerned about the maladies and the future of the world, they sometimes regard history as less relevant and less useful than other problem-related social sciences or activist fields of study. At a time when war, pollution, unemployment, crime, narcotics, and the generation gap confound American youth, what can history tell them? When tolerance and understanding are in short supply between the young and the old, the black and the white, the militant and the conservative, the study of the past may appear distressingly insignificant.

Actually, the notion that our dilemmas or our attempted solutions are unique is superficial, if not absurd. Our search for panaceas in the present must be informed by a knowledge of past times and places. The insights garnered from the way in which others handled their problems add an extra and necessary dimension to contemporary analysis.

The thirteen essays included in this volume deal with the panorama of human experience through an examination of the ingredients of everyday living in America: sex, race, taxes, and the appropriate role of women in society. Unfortunately, popular history has been a term with unsavory connotations because most works in this category are more popular than they are history. The essays within were selected on the basis of interest and readability, but they also represent the work of some of the most distinguished scholars in the United States. With this combination, it is hoped *American Vistas* will offer to the student an exciting, rich, and intelligent sampling of this nation's past.

Because we assume that this anthology will be used chiefly in conjunction with a survey textbook, we have focused upon questions and events generally lightly treated in the basic classroom volume. This has meant more attention to Puritan attitudes toward sex than Puritan attitudes toward God; the three-cornered relationship beween blacks, whites, and Indians rather than the usual two-sided analysis; and the character of Thomas Jefferson the man rather than Thomas Jefferson the philosopher and politician. At the same time, however, we recognize that the major topics dealt with in the basic text must also be illuminated here. Consequently we have included essays on slavery, the American Revolution, national expansion, the coming of the Civil War, and Reconstruction.

In such a short volume the problem of proportion has been especially difficult. Obviously all of the main issues in American history could not be included but we have tried to maintain a rough chronological and geographical balance. The essays do encompass a wide range of subjects, and each one is preceded by a brief introduction that places the selection in context and points out some of the more important questions which the article might raise. The complete citation is also included so that students seeking documentation may refer to the original source.

For aid in the selection of articles we wish to thank Professor William E. Leuchtenburg of Columbia University, and Professor William H. Hackett of Henry Ford Community College. Joseph A. Fineman and Christine Sharp assisted with the proofreading. Finally, we must acknowledge the substantial participation of Barbara Bruce Jackson at every stage of the compilation. She represented the intelligent nonprofessional historian in our deliberations and worked as an equal partner to help make our anthology both scholarly and literate.

Leonard Dinnerstein
University of Arizona

Kenneth T. Jackson
Columbia University

December 1970

CONTENTS

I AMERICAN BEGINNINGS
1607–1800

The Puritans and Sex

EDMUND S. MORGAN

• In 1630, after an arduous Atlantic crossing aboard the *Arabella*, John Winthrop and a small band of followers established the Massachusetts Bay Colony. In their "Holy Commonwealth" the Puritans emphasized hard work, severe discipline, and rigid self-examination and self-denial. Ministers had great political influence in the theocratic government, and profanation of the Sabbath day, blasphemy, fornication, drunkenness, and participation in games of chance or theatrical performances were among their many penal offenses. Even today the term "puritanical" suggests narrow-mindedness and excessive strictness in matters of morals and religion. Yet, as Daniel Boorstin and others have observed, the Puritans were not simply an ascetic group of fanatics who prohibited all earthly pleasures. Actually the severity of their code of behavior has frequently been exaggerated. The Puritans were subject to normal human desires and weaknesses, and they recognized that "the use of the marriage bed" is "founded in Man's nature." Moreover, numerous cases of fornication and adultery in the law courts of New England belie the notion that all Puritans lived up to their rigid moral ideology. In the following essay, Professor Edmund S. Morgan cites numerous examples of men and women, youths and maids, whose natural urges recognized no legal limits. In viewing their enforcement of laws and their judgments of human frailty, we may find that the Puritans do not always conform to their conventional stereotype as over-precise moralists.

From *New England Quarterly*, XV (1942), 591–607. Reprinted by permission of the author and the publisher.

Henry Adams once observed that Americans have "ostentatiously ignored" sex. He could think of only two American writers who touched upon the subject with any degree of boldness—Walt Whitman and Bret Harte. Since the time when Adams made this penetrating observation, American writers have been making up for lost time in a way that would make Bret Harte, if not Whitman, blush. And yet there is still more truth than falsehood in Adams's statement. Americans, by comparison with Europeans or Asiatics, are squeamish when confronted with the facts of life. My purpose is not to account for this squeamishness, but simply to point out that the Puritans, those bogeymen of the modern intellectual, are not responsible for it.

At the outset, consider the Puritans' attitude toward marriage and the role of sex in marriage. The popular assumption might be that the Puritans frowned on marriage and tried to hush up the physical aspect of it as much as possible, but listen to what they themselves had to say. Samuel Willard, minister of the Old South Church in the latter part of the seventeenth century and author of the most complete textbook of Puritan divinity, more than once expressed his horror at "that Popish conceit of the Excellency of Virginity." Another minister, John Cotton, wrote that

> Women are Creatures without which there is no comfortable Living for man: it is true of them what is wont to be said of Governments, *That bad ones are better than none*: They are a sort of Blasphemers then who dispise and decry them, and call them *a necessary Evil*, for they are *a necessary Good*.

These sentiments did not arise from an interpretation of marriage as a spiritual partnership, in which sexual intercourse was a minor or incidental matter. Cotton gave his opinion of "Platonic love" when he recalled the case of

> one who immediately upon marriage, without ever approaching the *Nuptial Bed*, indented with the *Bride*, that by mutual consent they might both live such a life, and according did sequestring themselves according to the custom of those times, from the rest of mankind, and afterwards from one another too, in their retired Cells, giving themselves up to a Contemplative life; and this is recorded as an instance of no little or ordinary Vertue; but I must be pardoned in it, if I can account it no other

than an effort of blind zeal, for they are the dictates of a blind
mind they follow therein, and not of that Holy Spirit, which
saith *It is not good that man should be alone.*

Here is as healthy an attitude as one could hope to find anywhere.
Cotton certainly cannot be accused of ignoring human nature. Nor
was he an isolated example among the Puritans. Another minister
stated plainly that "the Use of the Marriage Bed" is "founded in mans
Nature," and that consequently any withdrawal from sexual intercourse
upon the part of husband or wife "Denies all reliefe in Wedlock vnto
Human necessity: and sends it for supply vnto Beastiality when God
gives not the gift of Continency." In other words, sexual intercourse
was a human necessity and marriage the only proper supply for it.
These were the views of the New England clergy, the acknowledged
leaders of the community, the most Puritanical of the Puritans. As
proof that their congregations concurred with them, one may cite the
case in which the members of the First Church of Boston expelled
James Mattock because, among other offenses, "he denied Coniugall
fellowship vnto his wife for the space of 2 years together vpon pretense
of taking Revenge upon himself for his abusing of her before mar-
ryage." So strongly did the Puritans insist upon the sexual character
of marriage that one New Englander considered himself slandered
when it was reported, "that he Brock his deceased wife's hart with
Greife, that he would be absent from her 3 weeks together when he
was at home, and wold never come nere her, and such· Like."

There was just one limitation which the Puritans placed upon sexual relations in marriage: sex must not interfere with religion. Man's
chief end was to glorify God, and all earthly delights must promote
that end, not hinder it. Love for a wife was carried too far when it led
a man to neglect his God:

> . . . sometimes a man hath a good affection to Religion, but the
> love of his wife carries him away, a man may bee so transported
> to his wife, that hee dare not bee forward in Religion, lest hee
> displease his wife, and so the wife, lest shee displease her hus-
> band, and this is an inordinate love, when it exceeds measure.

Sexual pleasures, in this respect, were treated like other kinds of
pleasure. On a day of fast, when all comforts were supposed to be

foregone in behalf of religious contemplation, not only were tasty food and drink to be abandoned but sexual intercourse, too. On other occasions, when food, drink, and recreation were allowable, sexual intercourse was allowable too, though of course only between persons who were married to each other. The Puritans were not ascetics; they never wished to prevent the enjoyment of earthly delights. They merely demanded that the pleasures of the flesh be subordinated to the greater glory of God: husband and wife must not become "so transported with affection, that they look at no higher end than marriage it self." "Let such as have wives," said the ministers, "look at them not for their own ends, but to be fitted for Gods service, and bring them nearer to God."

Toward sexual intercourse outside marriage the Puritans were as frankly hostile as they were favorable to it in marriage. They passed laws to punish adultery with death, and fornication with whipping. Yet they had no misconceptions as to the capacity of human beings to obey such laws. Although the laws were commands of God, it was only natural—since the fall of Adam—for human beings to break them. Breaches must be punished lest the community suffer the wrath of God, but no offense, sexual or otherwise, could be occasion for surprise or for hushed tones of voice. How calmly the inhabitants of seventeenth-century New England could contemplate rape or attempted rape is evident in the following testimony offered before the Middlesex County Court of Massachusetts:

> The examination of Edward Wire taken the 7th of october and alsoe Zachery Johnson. who sayeth that Edward Wires mayd being sent into the towne about busenes meeting with a man that dogd hir from about Joseph Kettles house to goody marshes. She came into William Johnsones and desired Zachery Johnson to goe home with her for that the man dogd hir. accordingly he went with her and being then as far as Samuell Phips his house the man over tooke them. which man caled himselfe by the name of peter grant would have led the mayd but she oposed itt three times: and coming to Edward Wires house the said grant would have kist hir but she refused itt: wire being at prayer grant dragd the mayd between the said wiers and Nathanill frothinghams house. hee then flung the mayd downe in the streete and got atop hir; Johnson seeing it hee caled vppon the fellow to be sivill and not abuse the mayd then Edward wire came forth and ran to the said grant and took hold of him asking him what he did

to his mayd, the said grant asked whether she was his wife for he did nothing to his wife: the said grant swearing he would be the death of the said wire. when he came of the mayd; he swore he would bring ten men to pul down his house and soe ran away and they followed him as far as good[y] phipses house where they mett with John Terry and George Chin with clubs in there hands and soe they went away together. Zachy Johnson going to Constable Heamans, and wire going home. there came John Terry to his house to ask for beer and grant was in the streete but afterward departed into the towne, both Johnson and Wire both aferme that when grant was vppon the mayd she cryed out severall times.

Deborah hadlocke being examined sayth that she mett with the man that cals himselfe peeter grant about good prichards that he dogd hir and followed hir to hir masters and there threw hir downe and lay vppon hir but had not the use of hir body but swore several othes that he would ly with hir and gett hir with child before she got home.

Grant being present denys all saying he was drunk and did not know what he did.

The Puritans became inured to sexual offenses, because there were so many. The impression which one gets from reading the records of seventeenth-century New England courts is that illicit sexual intercourse was fairly common. The testimony given in cases of fornication and adultery—by far the most numerous class of criminal cases in the records—suggests that many of the early New Englanders possessed a high degree of virility and very few inhibitions. Besides the case of Peter Grant, take the testimony of Elizabeth Knight about the manner of Richard Nevars's advances toward her:

The last publique day of Thanksgiving (in the year 1674) in the evening as I was milking Richard Nevars came to me, and offered me abuse in putting his hand, under my coates, but I turning aside with much adoe, saved my self, and when I was settled to milking he agen took me by the shoulder and pulled me backward almost, but I clapped one hand on the Ground and held fast the Cows teatt with the other hand, and cryed out, and then came to mee Jonathan Abbot one of my Masters Servants, whome the said Never asked wherefore he came, the said Abbot said to look after you, what you doe unto the Maid, but the said Never bid Abbot goe about his businesse but I bade the lad to stay.

One reason for the abundance of sexual offenses was the number of men in the colonies who were unable to gratify their sexual desires in marriage. Many of the first settlers had wives in England. They had come to the new world to make a fortune, expecting either to bring their families after them or to return to England with some of the riches of America. Although these men left their wives behind, they brought their sexual appetites with them; and in spite of laws which required them to return to their families, they continued to stay, and more continued to arrive, as indictments against them throughout the seventeenth century clearly indicate.

Servants formed another group of men, and of women too, who could not ordinarily find supply for human necessity within the bounds of marriage. Most servants lived in the homes of their masters and could not marry without their consent, a consent which was not likely to be given unless the prospective husband or wife also belonged to the master's household. This situation will be better understood if it is recalled that most servants at this time were engaged by con- tract for a stated period. They were, in the language of the time, "covenant servants," who had agreed to stay with their masters for a number of years in return for a specified recompense, such as trans- portation to New England or education in some trade (the latter, of course, were known more specifically as apprentices). Even hired servants who worked for wages were usually single, for as soon as a man had enough money to buy or build a house of his own and to get married, he would set up in farming or trade for himself. It must be emphasized, however, that anyone who was not in business for him- self was necessarily a servant. The economic organization of seven- teenth-century New England had no place for the independent pro- letarian workman with a family of his own. All production was carried on in the household by the master of the family and his servants, so that most men were either servants or masters of servants; and the former, of course, were more numerous than the latter. Probably most of the inhabitants of Puritan New England could remember a time when they had been servants.

Theoretically no servant had a right to a private life. His time, day or night, belonged to his master, and both religion and law required that he obey his master scrupulously. But neither religion nor law could restrain the sexual impulses of youth, and if those impulses could not be expressed in marriage, they had to be given vent outside marriage. Servants had little difficulty in finding the occasions. Though they might be kept at work all day, it was easy enough to slip away at night. Once out of the house, there were several ways of meeting with a maid. The simplest way was to go to her bedchamber, if she was so fortunate as to have a private one of her own. Thus Jock, Mr. Solomon Phipps's Negro man, confessed in court

> that on the sixteenth day of May 1682, in the morning, betweene 12 and one of the clock, he did force open the back doores of the House of Laurence Hammond in Charlestowne, and came in to the House, and went up into the garret to Marie the Negro.
>
> He doth likewise acknowledge that one night the last week he forced into the House the same way, and went up to the Negro Woman Marie and that the like he hath done at severall other times before.

Joshua Fletcher took a more romantic way of visiting his lady:

> Joshua Fletcher . . . doth confesse and acknowledge that three severall nights, after bedtime, he went into Mr Fiskes Dwelling house at Chelmsford, at an open window by a ladder that he brought with him. the said windo opening into a chamber, whose was the lodging place of Gresill Juell servant to mr. Fiske. and there he kept company with the said mayd. she sometimes having her cloathes on, and one time he found her in her bed.

Sometimes a maidservant might entertain callers in the parlor while the family were sleeping upstairs. John Knight described what was perhaps a common experience for masters. The crying of his child awakened him in the middle of the night, and he called to his maid, one Sarah Crouch, who was supposed to be sleeping with the child. Receiving no answer, he arose and

> went downe the stayres, and at the stair foot, the latch of doore was pulled in. I called severall times and at the last said if shee would not open the dore, I would break it open, and when she opened the doore shee was all undressed and Sarah Largin with her undressed, also the said Sarah went out of doores and Dropped some of her clothes as shee went out. I enquired of Sarah Crouch what men they were, which was with them. Shee made mee no answer for some space of time, but at last shee told me Peeter Brigs was with them, I asked her whether Thomas Jones was not there, but shee would give mee no answer.

In the temperate climate of New England it was not always necessary to seek out a maid at her home. Rachel Smith was seduced in an open field "about nine of the clock at night, being darke, neither moone nor starrs shineing." She was walking through the field when she met a man who

> asked her where shee lived, and what her name was and shee told him. and then shee asked his name, and he told her Saijing that he was old Good-man Shepards man. Also shee saith he gave her strong liquors, and told her that it was not the first time he had been with maydes after his master was in bed.

Sometimes, of course, it was not necessary for a servant to go outside his master's house in order to satisfy his sexual urges. Many cases of fornication are on record between servants living in the same house. Even where servants had no private bedroom, even where the whole family slept in a single room, it was not impossible to make love. In fact many love affairs must have had their consummation upon a bed in which other people were sleeping. Take for example the case of Sarah Lepingwell. When Sarah was brought into court for having an illegitimate child, she related that one night when her master's brother, Thomas Hawes, was visiting the family, she went to bed early. Later, after Hawes had gone to bed, he called to her to get him a pipe of tobacco. After refusing for some time,

> at the last I arose and did lite his pipe and cam and lay doune one my one bead and smoaked about half the pip and siting vp in my bead to giue him his pip my bead being a trundell bead at the sid of his bead he reached beyond the pip and Cauth me by the wrist and pulled me on the side of his bead but I biding him let me goe he bid me hold my peas the folks wold here me and if it be replyed come why did you not call out I Ansar I was posesed with fear of my mastar least my mastar shold think I did it only to bring a scandall on his brothar and thinking thay wold all beare witnes agaynst me but the thing is true that he did then begete me with child at that tim and the Child is Thomas Hauses and noe mans but his.

In his defense Hawes offered the testimony of another man who was sleeping "on the same side of the bed," but the jury nevertheless accepted Sarah's story.

The fact that Sarah was intimidated by her master's brother suggests that maidservants may have been subject to sexual abuse by their masters. The records show that sometimes masters did take advantage of their position to force unwanted attentions upon their female servants. The case of Elizabeth Dickerman is a good example. She complained to the Middlesex County Court,

> against her master John Harris senior for profiring abus to her by way of forsing her to be naught with him: . . . he has tould her that if she tould her dame: what cariag he did show to her shee had as good be hanged and shee replyed then shee would run away and he sayd run the way is befor you: . . . she says if she should liwe ther shee shall be in fear of her lif.

The court accepted Elizabeth's complaint and ordered her master to be whipped twenty stripes.

So numerous did cases of fornication and adultery become in seventeenth-century New England that the problem of caring for the children of extra-marital unions was a serious one. The Puritans solved it, but in such a way as to increase rather than decrease the temptation to sin. In 1668 the General Court of Massachusetts ordered:

> that where any man is legally convicted to be the Father of a Bastard childe, he shall be at the care and charge to maintain and bring up the same, by such assistance of the Mother as nature requireth, and as the Court from time to time (according to circumstances) shall see meet to Order: and in case the Father of a Bastard, by confession or other manifest proof, upon trial of the case, do not appear to the Courts satisfaction, then the Man charged by the Woman to be the Father, shee holding constant in it, (especially being put upon the real discovery of the truth of it in the time of her Travail) shall be the reputed Father, and accordingly be liable to the charge of maintenance as aforesaid (though not to other punishment) notwithstanding his denial, unless the circumstances of the case and pleas be such, on the behalf of the man charged, as that the Court that have the cognizance thereon shall see reason to acquit him, and otherwise dispose of the Childe and education thereof.

As a result of this law a girl could give way to temptation without the fear of having to care for an illegitimate child by herself. Furthermore, she could, by a little simple lying, spare her lover the expense of sup-

porting the child. When Elizabeth Wells bore a child, less than a year
after this statute was passed, she laid it to James Tufts, her master's
son. Goodman Tufts affirmed that Andrew Robinson, servant to Goodman Dexter, was the real father, and he brought the following testimony as evidence:

> Wee Elizabeth Jefts aged 15 ears and Mary tufts aged 14 ears
> doe testyfie that their being one at our hous sumtime the last
> winter who sayed that thear was a new law made concerning
> bastards that If aney man wear aqused with a bastard and the
> woman which had aqused him did stand vnto it in her labor that
> he should bee the reputed father of it and should mayntaine it
> Elizabeth Wells hearing of the sayd law she sayed vnto vs that
> If shee should bee with Child shee would bee sure to lay it vn to
> won who was rich enough abell to mayntayne it wheather it wear
> his or no and shee farder sayed Elizabeth Jefts would not you doe
> so likewise If it weare your case and I sayed no by no means for
> right must tacke place: and the sayd Elizabeth wells sayed If it
> wear my Caus I think I should doe so.

A tragic unsigned letter that somehow found its way into the files of
the Middlesex County Court gives more direct evidence of the practice which Elizabeth Wells professed:

> der loue i remember my loue to you hoping your welfar and i
> hop to imbras the but now i rit to you to let you nowe that i am
> a child by you and i wil ether kil it or lay it to an other and you
> shal have no blame at al for I haue had many children and none
> have none of them. . . . [i.e., none of their fathers is support-
> ing any of them.]

In face of the wholesale violation of the sexual codes to which all
these cases give testimony, the Puritans could not maintain the severe penalties which their laws provided. Although cases of adultery
occurred every year, the death penalty is not known to have been
applied more than three times. The usual punishment was a whipping
or a fine, or both, and perhaps a branding, combined with a symbolical
execution in the form of standing on the gallows for an hour with a
rope about the neck. Fornication met with a lighter whipping or a
lighter fine, while rape was treated in the same way as adultery. Though
the Puritans established a code of laws which demanded perfection—

which demanded, in other words, strict obedience to the will of God,
they nevertheless knew that frail human beings could never live up to
the code. When fornication, adultery, rape, or even buggery and sodomy appeared, they were not surprised, nor were they so severe with
the offenders as their codes of law would lead one to believe. Sodomy,
to be sure, they usually punished with death; but rape, adultery, and
fornication they regarded as pardonable human weaknesses, all the
more likely to appear in a religious community, where the normal
course of sin was stopped by wholesome laws. Governor Bradford, in
recounting the details of an epidemic of sexual misdemeanors in Plym-
outh, wrote resignedly:

> it may be in this case as it is with waters when their streames are
> stopped or damned up, when they gett passage they flow with
> more violence, and make more noys and disturbance, then when
> they are suffered to rune quietly in their owne chanels. So wick-
> ednes being here more stopped by strict laws, and the same more
> nerly looked unto, so as it cannot rune in a comone road of liberty
> as it would, and is inclined, it searches every wher, and at last
> breaks out wher it getts vente.

The estimate of human capacities here expressed led the Puritans
not only to deal leniently with sexual offenses but also to take every
precaution to prevent such offenses, rather than wait for the necessity
of punishment. One precaution was to see that children got married
as soon as possible. The wrong way to promote virtue, the Puritans
thought, was to "ensnare" children in vows of virginity, as the Cath-
olics did. As a result of such vows, children, "not being able to con-
tain," would be guilty of "unnatural pollutions, and other filthy practices in secret: and too oft of horrid Murthers of the fruit of their
bodies," said Thomas Cobbett. The way to avoid fornication and per-
version was for parents to provide suitable husbands and wives for
their children:

> Lot was to blame that looked not out seasonably for some fit
> matches for his two daughters, which had formerly minded mar-
> riage (witness the contract between them and two men in *Sodom*,
> called therfore for his Sons in Law, which had married his
> daughters, Gen. 19. 14.) for they seeing no man like to come into
> them in a conjugall way . . . then they plotted that incestuous
> course, whereby their Father was so highly dishonoured. . . .

As marriage was the way to prevent fornication, successful marriage was the way to prevent adultery. The Puritans did not wait for adultery to appear; instead, they took every means possible to make husbands and wives live together and respect each other. If a husband deserted his wife and remained within the jurisdiction of a Puritan government, he was promptly sent back to her. Where the wife had been left in England, the offense did not always come to light until the wayward husband had committed fornication or bigamy, and of course there must have been many offenses which never came to light. But where both husband and wife lived in New England, neither had much chance of leaving the other without being returned by order of the county court at its next sitting. When John Smith of Medfield left his wife and went to live with Patience Rawlins, he was sent home poorer by ten pounds and richer by thirty stripes. Similarly Mary Drury, who deserted her husband on the pretense that he was impotent, failed to convince the court that he actually was so, and had to return to him as well as to pay a fine of five pounds. The wife of Phillip Pointing received lighter treatment: when the court thought that she had overstayed her leave in Boston, they simply ordered her "to depart the Towne and goe to Tanton to her husband." The courts, moreover, were not satisfied with mere cohabitation; they insisted that it be peaceful cohabitation. Husbands and wives were forbidden by law to strike one another, and the law was enforced on numerous occasions. But the courts did not stop there. Henry Flood was required to give bond for good behavior because he had abused his wife simply by "ill words calling her whore and cursing of her." The wife of Christopher Collins was presented for railing at her husband and calling him "Gurley gutted divill." Apparently in this case the court thought that Mistress Collins was right, for although the fact was proved by two witnesses, she was discharged. On another occasion the court favored the husband: Jacob Pudeator, fined for striking and kicking his wife, had the sentence moderated when the court was informed that she was a woman "of great provocation."

Wherever there was strong suspicion that an illicit relation might arise between two persons, the authorities removed the temptation by forbidding the two to come together. As early as November, 1630, the Court of Assistants of Massachusetts prohibited a Mr. Clark from "cohabitacion and frequent keepeing company with Mrs. Freeman, vnder paine of such punishment as the Court shall thinke meete to inflict." Mr. Clark and Mr. Freeman were both bound "in XX£ apeece that Mr. Clearke shall make his personall appearance att the nexte Court to be holden in March nexte, and in the meane tyme to carry himselfe in good behaviour towards all people and espetially towards Mrs. Freeman, concerning whome there is stronge suspicion of incontinency." Forty-five years later the Suffolk County Court took the same kind of measure to protect the husbands of Dorchester from the temptations offered by the daughter of Robert Spurr: Spurr was presented by the grand jury

> for entertaining persons at his house at unseasonable times both by day and night to the greife of theire wives and Relations &c The Court having heard what was alleaged and testified against him do Sentence him to bee admonish't and to pay Fees of Court and charge him upon his perill not to entertain any married men to keepe company with his daughter especially James Minott and Joseph Belcher.

In like manner Walter Hickson was forbidden to keep company with Mary Bedwell, "And if at any time hereafter hee bee taken in company of the saide Mary Bedwell without other company to bee forthwith apprehended by the Constable and to be whip't with ten stripes." Elizabeth Wheeler and Joanna Peirce were admonished "for theire disorderly carriage in the house of Thomas Watts being married women and founde sitting in other mens Laps with theire Armes about theire Necks." How little confidence the Puritans had in human nature is even more clearly displayed by another case, in which Edmond Maddock and his wife were brought to court "to answere to all such matters as shalbe objected against them concerning Haarkwoody and Ezekiell Euerells being at their house at unseasonable tyme of the night and her being up with them after her husband was gone to bed." Haarkwoody and Everell had been found "by the Constable Henry Bridghame about tenn of the Clock at night sitting by the fyre at the house of Edmond Maddocks with his wyfe a suspicious weoman her husband being on sleepe [*sic*] on the bedd." A similar distrust of human ability to resist temptation is evident in the following order of the Connecticut Particular Court:

James Hallett is to returne from the Correction house to his master Barclyt, who is to keepe him to hard labor, and course dyet during the pleasure of the Court provided that Barclet is first to remove his daughter from his family, before the sayd James enter therein.

These precautions, as we have already seen, did not eliminate fornication, adultery, or other sexual offenses, but they doubtless reduced the number from what it would otherwise have been.

In sum, the Puritan attitude toward sex, though directed by a belief in absolute, God-given moral values, never neglected human nature. The rules of conduct which the Puritans regarded as divinely ordained had been formulated for men, not for angels and not for beasts. God had created mankind in two sexes; He had ordained marriage as desirable for all, and sexual intercourse as essential to marriage. On the other hand, He had forbidden sexual intercourse outside of marriage. These were the moral principles which the Puritans sought to enforce in New England. But in their enforcement they took cognizance of human nature. They knew well enough that human beings since the fall of Adam were incapable of obeying perfectly the laws of God. Consequently, in the endeavor to enforce those laws they treated offenders with patience and understanding, and concentrated their efforts on prevention more than on punishment. The result was not a society in which most of us would care to live, for the methods of prevention often caused serious interference with personal liberty. It must nevertheless be admitted that in matters of sex the Puritans showed none of the blind zeal or narrow-minded bigotry which is too often supposed to have been characteristic of them. The more one learns about these people, the less do they appear to have resembled the sad and sour portraits which their modern critics have drawn of them.

Divide and Rule: Red, White, and Black in the Southeast

WILLIAM S. WILLIS

• Racial thought is as old as civilized man. It has been a part of European and Oriental culture since antiquity, and its elements have existed in India, China, Egypt, Palestine, and Greece. It is hardly surprising that the United States has always been a racist society; the earliest colonists simply brought with them to the American continent the attitudes and prejudices that prevailed in Europe in their day. The English, for example, considered themselves to be God's chosen people and thought of men of different skin color as being inferior.

In the colonial period white settlers found themselves in a minority position with regard to the blacks and the Indians in the Southeast. Fearful that the two groups might combine against them, the whites made every effort to turn Negroes and Indians against each other. In this way, the European settlers hoped to preserve order and retain white supremacy in the New World. That they succeeded in their task we know. Whether their actions were morally justified is another question.

North of Mexico, the Colonial Southeast was the only place where Indians, Whites, and Negroes met in large numbers. Little of the fascinating story of this contact has been told and some crucial parts may be beyond recall for lack of documents. The early attitude of Indians toward Negroes is obviously of great importance. To some extent, it has been dealt with, but conclusions have differed. Laurence

From *Journal of Negro History*, 48 (1962), 157–76. Copyright © 1962 by ASNLH. Reprinted by permission of the Association for the Study of Negro Life and History.

Foster and James Johnston are certain that the early feeling of Indians was one of friendliness. On the other hand, some students, mainly Southern historians, stress hostility. As a matter of fact, a great deal of hostility seems to have existed in the eighteenth century. In 1752, the Catawba Indians showed great anger and bitter resentment when a Negro came among them as a trader. Perhaps the Cherokee had the strongest color prejudice of all Indians. Even the Spaniards were not "White" enough for them. In 1793, Little Turkey, a prominent chief, declared that Spaniards were not "real white people, and what few I have seen of them looked like mulattoes, and I would never have anything to say to them." According to John Brickell, an early eighteenth century reporter, Indians had a "natural aversion to the Blacks." In 1763, George Milligen Johnston, a South Carolina physician, opined that this hostility was mutual and spoke of the "natural Dislike and Antipathy, that subsists between them [Negroes] and our *Indian* Neighbors." But the Southern historians have not explained why Indians disliked Negroes. This paper examines this hostility, and that of Negroes to Indians. The story is the familiar one of divide and rule. Specifically, it will be shown that Whites willfully helped create the antagonism between Indians and Negroes in order to preserve themselves and their privileges.

In the Colonial Southeast, Negro slavery and trade with Indians were more prominent in South Carolina than anywhere else. The province sanctioned slavery from its beginnings in 1670, but South Carolinians brought in few Negroes until the late 1690's. From that time, the steady increase in the number of Negro slaves correlates with the steadily increasing demand for labor. First, there was the expansion of rice production on slave-operated plantations. This occurred at about the same time, near the turn of the eighteenth century, that the general supply of slaves in the New World swelled. In the 1720's, the manufacture of pitch and tar, and in the 1740's the growth of indigo production added to the demand for slave labor. Meanwhile other events conspired to curtail other supplies of labor. Indian slavery dwindled and virtually disappeared after the Yamassee War of 1715-1717. This rebellion of tribes trading with the province produced a widespread notion that South Carolina was a dangerous place and few Whites entered for two decades after the fighting. The demand for Negroes grew in tandem with the mounting political power of the planters and the government was increasingly responsive to the latter's demands. By the beginning of the eighteenth century, Negroes outnumbered Whites and they increased their proportion of the population later in the century when various estimates put the ratio at two or three to one and even higher.

Despite allegations about the submissiveness of Negroes and their acquiescence to slavery, eighteenth century Whites were afraid of their slaves. This fear grew as Negroes became more numerous. Whites especially dreaded slave insurrections; to South Carolinians, Negro rebels were an "intestine Enemy the most dreadful of Enemies." The eighteenth century was punctuated by a steady succession of insurrectionary plots and actual insurrections. Indeed, the Charles Town government at times kept half of its soldiers in the capital. Negroes also struck back at their masters in other ways. They poisoned them, they set fires, and they committed suicide. They also employed subtle everyday resistances, such as, malingering and feigned stupidity. They also ran away. Some went for only short periods to nearby places; others went permanently to distant hiding places, to the mountains and swamps, to the Indian country, and to the Spanish in Florida. Running south to Florida became especially common after the Yamassee War when Spain encouraged more Negroes to come and offered them freedom. By the late 1720's, Negro subversion had become the main defense problem of South Carolina.

Indians were also a big problem, and they were feared. The Colonial Southeast was an arena of an unremitting struggle for empire among Whites: English, French, Spanish, and later Americans. Indian tribes were caught in the middle of this struggle; and Whites competed for their allegiance, for their trade and their warriors. Success in the empire struggle depended upon success in the Indian country. For a decade at least, the mere survival of South Carolina remained uncertain and the position of the province among Indians was precarious. But even before the eighteenth century, South Carolina had become much more secure and had constructed a remarkable system of Indian alliances. These alliances gave South Carolina sway over the majority of Indians in the South and forced the Spanish and French to keep retreating. Through its successes, South Carolina became confident, perhaps overconfident, of controlling Indians. Then came the Yamassee War. For a time South Carolinians were on the verge of being driven into the sea; however, in the end they had their victory. But with all the devastation, their province emerged from the war weakened and insecure, with Spain and France stronger than ever. The old confidence of managing Indians was gone, and gone for good. They now believed more than ever that Indians could never be really trusted. From now on, they and all Whites lived in dread of the next Indian uprising—an uprising that would be supported by enemy Whites.

The picture in the Colonial Southeast was this: a frightened and dominant White minority faced two exploited colored majorities. To meet the Negro danger, South Carolina devised a harsh slave code; the police control of slaves was comprehensive, specific, and brutal. To meet the Indian danger, the province had a system of trade regulation that was less brutal than the slave code but of approximately equal thoroughness. That Indian tribes were still independent and had some freedom of choice necessitated their being dealt with somewhat like equals. After the Yamassee War, the province played tribe off against tribe; indeed, village against village. They also watched the munitions trade to prevent any stockpiling of arms. In meeting each danger, South Carolinians were plagued by the discrepancy between what they willed and what they could actually do. This discrepancy became greater with time. It did not take much imagination on the part of Whites to put the two dangers, Indians and Negro slaves, together. As early as 1712, Governor Alexander Spotswood, of Virginia, juxtaposed them. In 1729, the French delayed sending an expedition against the Natchez Indians who had slaughtered French citizens because they feared that New Orleans without troops would be attacked by the Choctaw Indians, and Negroes in order to "free themselves from slavery, might join them." This was the biggest fear of all. In 1775, John Stuart, British Superintendent of Southern Indian Affairs, explained that "nothing can be more alarming to Carolinians than the idea of an attack from Indians and Negroes."

What did South Carolinians do about this nightmare? One answer was, keep Indians and Negroes apart—do not let them mix. In 1757, Captain Daniel Pepper, agent to the Creek Indians, stated that "intimacy" between Indians and Negroes should be avoided. In 1767, Stuart expressed this idea again, perhaps even more strongly: "any Intercourse between Indians and Negroes in my opinion ought to be prevented as much as possible." If this were done, Negroes could not establish personal relations with Indians and learn their languages. This would eliminate the dreaded coordinated blow by Indians and Negroes. But Whites also had other goals in mind. Whites believed that whenever Negro and Indian talked in private the talk was against them. The government believed that Negroes could spread discontent among the tribes and foil its schemes in the Indian country. In 1779, the British Indian Service stated that "Negroes infused many very bad notions into their [Indians] minds." To do this, Negroes need not always lie; as servants, they were sometimes privy to important secrets. Moreover, the government *was* double-dealing with its Indian allies; for instance, stirring up trouble between Creeks and Cherokee. On the other hand, Indians could offer freedom to Negroes and tell them how to get to their villages.

To this end of keeping these colored peoples apart, South Carolinians tried to prevent Indians from coming into the province unless they were on official business. In 1742, a Committee on Indian Affairs warned against frequent visiting by Indians because of the hazard of their associating with slaves, "particularly in regard to their talking, and having too great Intercourse with our Slaves, at the out-plantations, where they camp." Even when on official missions to Charles Town, chiefs were discouraged from bringing too many *aides-de-camp* and were hurried away as quickly as possible. The Settlement Indians, those partially detribalized natives living within the province, presented a special problem. Here again the government opposed contact with Negroes; trading and intermarriage were frowned upon. This determination to prevent Indian-Negro contacts within the White settlements was a main cause for curtailing the enslavement of Indians. Indian slaves got to know Negroes and, since they escaped easily into the hinterland, they might carry Negroes along with them. In 1729, Governor Etienne Perier, of Louisiana, explained that "Indian slaves being mixed with our negroes may induce them to desert."

Keeping Negroes and Indians apart had another aim: keep Negroes out of the Indian country. Eighteenth century legislation consistently prohibited any Negro, slave or free, from going to any Indian tribe either as a trader in his own right or as a White trader's helper. Violations of this prohibition almost always led to hasty action to remove these Negroes. Later in the eighteenth century when the westward movement was getting into high gear, opposition to Whites taking their slaves into Indian country became an important obstruction to White settlement of the interior.

Fugitive Negroes among the Indians were the biggest headache. In 1767, Stuart declared that "to prevent the Indian Country [from] becoming an Asylum for Negroes is a Matter of the Utmost consequence to the prosperity of the provinces." To keep slaves from escaping, South Carolina assigned patrols to watch the roads and countryside; to keep Indian raiding parties out of the province, the government built forts at key approaches and sent rangers out to ride along the frontiers. But Indians were excellent slave catchers. The Settlement Indians in particular were regularly employed to track down fugitive slaves; indeed, slave catching was so profitable to them that they readily agreed in 1727 to move their villages so that they could do a better job. Whites went to great lengths to get their Negroes back. In negotiations, they pressed Indians about these fugitives. They made threats. In 1773, David Taitt, Indian agent, threatened to cut off the Creek trade unless the Indians returned fugitive Negroes. Most treaties stipulated that Indians surrender all Negroes and return all future runaways at an agreed price. Moreover, traders were required to report all Negroes found among Indians and to hold them until they could be sent back to their masters. On their tours of duty, Indian agents also watched for Negroes, and sometimes they made special trips into the Indian country to regain these fugitives.

Keeping Negroes and Indians apart had still another aim: keep Negroes out of the swamps and the mountains. Negroes frequently escaped to these out of the way places. These fugitives, called Maroons, preferred the swamps, especially those in the direction of St. Augustine. Their preference for the southern swamps was dictated by the prospect of freedom among the Spanish in Florida. Meanwhile in these swamps, they could expect help from the Spanish and their Indians. Probably this explains why they went less often to the Southern Appalachians, northwest of Charles Town. But sometimes fugitive Negroes did try for these mountains; for instance, fifteen from Virginia did this in 1729. Large parts of these mountains were impregnable from the east; indeed, South Carolinians realized they could never annihilate the Cherokee in these mountains and they feared that Maroons might team up with these Indians, who were becoming less friendly to the

English and more inclined to the French. If this occurred, the dispersed and almost defenceless White settlers on the Northwest frontier would be at the mercy of a truly formidable antagonist. On the other hand, if the Cherokee were driven from their villages, Maroons might occupy them and become prosperous and secure. These considerations weighed heavily with the Charles Town government, and they were important in leading this government to a policy of appeasing the Cherokee.

Maroons were the most resourceful of all fugitives. They aimed at nothing less than setting up small self-sufficient societies in the most inhospitable places. They had to plan ahead, carefully and secretly. They knew a hard life of hard work and hard fighting awaited them. Those fifteen Virginia Maroons carried guns, ammunition, clothing, furniture, and implements into the mountains; before they were captured, they had started clearing land in order to farm. Once established in their fastnesses, Maroons then lived as banditti; they plundered White settlements, killing masters and rescuing slaves. In 1717, a band under the leadership of one Sebastian terrorized the southern parishes of South Carolina. In the early 1770's, a frightened William Bartram, the noted naturalist, encountered a band of marauders north of Charles Town and later explained that "people [were] . . . frequently attacked, robbed, and sometimes murdered" by Negro bands in this region. These Maroons were dangerous men and women, and they struck out against slavery. No threat, however, was greater than the possibility of their cooperating with hostile Indians and coordinating their attacks against White settlements. Top priority was given by Whites to the immediate destruction of the Maroons. This job was too important to be handled by a local community. Instead the government sent soldiers into the wilderness to eliminate them. Indians were also called upon to help, and they were especially good at ferreting out Maroons from their lurking places.

In addition to keeping Indians and Negroes apart, Whites pitted the colored groups against each other. In 1725, Richard Ludlam, a South Carolina minister, confessed that "we make use of a Wile for our prest. Security to make Indians & Negro's a checque upon each other least by their Vastly Superior Numbers we should be crushed by one or the other." How did Whites go about this? The essential thing was to make bad blood between them: create suspicion, fear, and hatred. In 1758, James Glen, long governor of South Carolina, explained to William Lyttelton, his inexperienced successor, that "it has been allways the policy of this govert to creat an aversion in them [Indians] to Negroes."

It is difficult to show specifically how Whites went about creating this aversion. Eighteenth century Whites, and especially South Carolinians, were reluctant to write about these things. In 1775, when the American Revolution had already made slaveholders in South Carolina insecure, Colonel Stephen Bull wrote Colonel Henry Laurens about a scheme to create Indian-Negro aversion; but first he dismissed his secretary and wrote this part of his letter in his own hand, admonishing Laurens to keep this scheme secret from all South Carolinians except for a few high officials in the government.

Whites sought to convince Indians that Negroes worked against their best interests. In October, 1715, the Cherokee were on the verge of deserting their Indian confederates in the Yamessee War and joining South Carolina in an attack upon the Creeks. They hoped for a better trade with Charles Town and more security in the South. However, two runaway Negroes from South Carolina came to the Cherokee villages and, according to the South Carolinians, told these Indians a "parcell of lies" which dissuaded the Cherokee from joining the South Carolinians. Later in January, 1716, the Cherokee finally went over to the province; on their part, the South Carolinians agreed to specific commitments for a larger trade at cheap prices and for military support against all enemies of the Cherokee. For a while, it seemed that the province really intended to live up to these commitments and the Cherokee were happy with their new friends in Charles Town. During this time, Whites lost no chance of reminding the Indians that Negroes had almost prevented this boon from coming their way. Negroes were also made out to be dangerous people who would bring hardship and suffering to Indians. In 1739, a smallpox epidemic broke out among the Cherokee and about one thousand warriors died from the disease and from suicide because of their disfigurement. These Indians despaired so much that they lost confidence in their gods, and the priests destroyed the sacred objects of the tribe. Whites blamed the epidemic on Negroes, telling the Indians that new slaves from Africa had brought the disease to Charles Town. Since this was not the only epidemic that occurred in the Indian country, we may wonder if Whites had on other occasions also shifted the blame to Negroes.

Whites also contributed to this aversion by using Negro slaves as soldiers against Indians. These slaves were rewarded with goods and sometimes with their freedom. Negroes made good soldiers against other Negroes in rebellion; if they did this against their own people, they certainly had no compunction about fighting Indians. In the Yamassee War, trusted Negroes were drafted and armed and then sent against enemy Indians in the province. Later they were also used against enemy Indians in the interior. When South Carolina invaded the Cherokee country in 1715, Captain Stephen Ford commanded a Negro company. After the Cherokee had come to terms with the province, Ford's company remained in the Cherokee country and took part in attacking the Creeks. In fact, Cherokee chiefs requested this: they said that Negro soldiers would be "very seweasabell [serviceable] to them in Roning after ye Enimy." The French army that invaded the Chickasaw country in 1736 included a company of Negro slaves commanded by a free Negro named Simon; indeed, Simon distinguished himself under fire and was commended by the French. Nevertheless, Whites were reluctant to put muskets in the hands of their slaves; they did not do this until driven by desperation. But in emergencies they were always prepared to do so: legislation was passed in South Carolina in 1747, and renewed from time to time, that authorized the drafting of slaves so long as they did not exceed one third the number of White soldiers. Something besides desperation was behind this: Whites were telling Indians not to count on Negroes in planning another great uprising. This made for Indian antagonism. During the Second Natchez War in 1729, the French accused some Negro slaves of plotting insurrection with the Chouacha Indians, a small harmless tribe living near New Orleans. Although the accusation was unfounded, they armed the Negroes and ordered them to attack this tribe as the sole means of saving their own skins. An on-the-spot reporter tells us that "this expedition rendered the Indians [in Louisiana] mortal enemies of the negroes."

Employing Indians as slave catchers encouraged anti-Negro sentiment among the Indians themselves. Whites paid Indians well for returning fugitive slaves; for instance, at the great Augusta Conference in 1763, the price was set at one musket and three blankets for each slave brought in. The Indian trade was largely based on deerskins, and these skins were sold cheaply to the traders; in order to buy a musket and three blankets, an Indian had to pay about thirty-five skins. This required several months of hunting. Moreover, the hunting grounds were dangerous places; enemies were always lurking about. Hence, an Indian often lost time fighting, if we were lucky enough not to lose his life. In a word, Indians were usually short of goods and in debt. The reward for fugitive slaves was, therefore, something they could rarely afford to turn down. Moreover, the avariciousness of Indians was proverbial in the South. But Indians knew what slavery was like among Whites. They saw its cruelty and brutality whenever they visited the White settlements. They also remembered that Whites had once enslaved Indians in large numbers and occasionally still did so. Indeed, the great fear of Indians was that Whites, and especially South Carolinians, would at some time make slaves of all Indians in the South. This fear was in the background of all their dealings with Whites. All of this worked in two contradictory ways on Indians. Self-interest made the Indian act as an enemy of Negro freedom; but human feelings made him guilty. Like other men in this ambivalence, he suppressed his guilt with a convenient hostility.

Since it was important that Negroes should fear and hate Indians, it is likely that Whites told their slaves many horror stories about Indians, especially those depicting the terrible things that Indians did to Negroes. Actually it was not difficult to portray Indians in a bad light. Indians did kill and they were cruel. Sometimes their raiding parties striking swiftly and with surprise killed Negroes alongside their White masters. Indians also scalped and otherwise mutilated their victims regardless of race. Besides, Indians were known in the early days to subject their male captives to prolonged and deadly tortures; now and then they did this even in the eighteenth century. In 1730, the French gave the Choctaw three Negroes who had helped the Natchez in 1729. The French expected the Choctaw to torture these Negroes; moreover, they hoped this would discourage Negroes from cooperating with Indians. The French were not disappointed. Father Petit, a Jesuit missionary, reported that these Negroes "have been burned alive with a degree of cruelty which has inspired all the Negroes with a new horror of the Savages, which will have a beneficial effect in securing the safety of the colony." But atrocities were not the main thing. The main thing was that Indians often behaved as real enemies of Negro freedom. To a large extent, Whites encouraged Indians to act this way. As we shall see, this was partly done to make Negroes fear and hate Indians. Given this aim, we assume that Whites publicized these unfriendly acts of Indians among their slaves—and conveniently overlooked their own responsibility. We will now give attention to some situations in which Indians behaved as enemies of Negro freedom.

As we know, Whites employed Indians as slave catchers, and Indians were eager for these jobs. Moreover, Negroes knew that Indians, being expert woodsmen, were better slave catchers than White soldiers and patrols. Negroes also realized that death sometimes awaited the unsuccessful runaway instead of a return to slavery. The Charles Town government executed leaders of fugitive slave parties and those slaves who ran away repeatedly. This government also instructed slave catchers to kill fugitive Negroes when they could not capture them; therefore, dead fugitives were paid for as well as live ones. This encouraged Indians to be more bloodthirsty than White slave catchers: the labor of these fugitives was not going to benefit them. Besides, scalping was more profitable to them than to Whites: Indians could make one scalp look like two or more scalps. To prevent this cheating, the Charles Town government tried to buy only scalps with two ears. Bloodthirstiness was a particular characteristic of Settlement Indians, for slave catching was almost the only opportunity of recapturing the excitement of their old culture. The enthusiasm and violence of Indian slave catchers, as well as the dread Negroes had for them, have been forcibly described by Brickell: "As soon as the Indians have Notice from the *Christians* of their [slaves] being there [in the woods], they disperse them; killing some, others flying for Mercy to the *Christians* . . . rather than fall into the others [Indians] Hands . . . [who] put them to death with the most exquisite Tortures they can invent, whenever they catch them." It is not surprising that a Committee on Indian Affairs in 1727 instructed the Indian Commissioners to have "any Negroe or Negroes Corrected who shall threaten the [Settlement] Indians for Executing any Orders that the said Commissioners shall see fit to give the Indians." Whites did not employ Indians as slave catchers only to recover valuable property and to punish offenders. They also employed them to make their slaves hate Indians. In 1776, some Maroons established themselves on Tybee Island; the Charles Town government secretly arranged for Creek slave catchers to kill these Maroons. Colonel Stephen Bull explained that this would "establish a hatred or aversion between Indians and Negroes."

Indians also permitted and even helped Whites round up Negroes in and about the Indian villages. These Negroes were then conveyed back to slavery. This was a hard blow. These runaways had eluded all the slave catchers and then experienced the intoxication of freedom among the Indians. In either case, Indians betrayed them, blasting villages before moving on to Florida; other runaways settled down in these villages and started making some kind of life for themselves among the Indians. In either case, Indians betrayed them, blasting their hopes. Moreover, these Indians were betraying their own principles of hospitality and sanctuary for strangers—and these principles applied to fugitive Negroes. It seems that Indians, in their greed for trade goods, sometimes betrayed the same fugitives twice. After returning Negroes and collecting their reward, Indians helped these fugitives to escape again before White agents delivered them to their masters. Then these Indians recaptured these fugitives and demanded another full reward from the agents. In time, fugitive Negroes realized that they stayed in jeopardy while among Indians. In 1758, James Beamer, an old Cherokee trader, warned Governor Lyttelton to be discreet in sending for some runaways "for they are always on their Watch and the Least mistrust they have they Will fly Directly to the Woods." In retrieving fugitive slaves from the Indian country, Whites again had the additional motive of making Negroes antagonistic to Indians. Indeed, this motive at times made Whites willingly forego repossessing their slaves. It seems that Whites were pleased when Indians scalped fugitive slaves who lived in Indian villages but would not peaceably surrender. This happened among the Creeks in 1768; Stuart then explained that "this cannot fail of having a very good Effect, by breaking that Intercourse between Negroes & Savages which might have been attended with very troublesome consequences had it continued."

Indians were *bona fide* slave traders. They stole Negroes from White slaveholders in order to sell them to other White slaveholders. Indians had been prepared for this Negro trade by the earlier trade in Indian slaves; for instance, they had learned that male captives were often too valuable to be done away with. Except for raids by Spanish Indians against South Carolina, Indians did not steal too many Negroes in the first half of the eighteenth century. About the only other Indians that regularly raided for Negro slaves were the Chickasaw and other allied tribes of South Carolina living near the Mississippi River. These tribes raided French settlements in Louisiana and French convoys on the Great River. Negroes captured in these raids were sold to Charles Town traders who carried them to South Carolina. This trade did not bring many slaves into the province; the French were always so short of Negroes. For the Negroes, this trade was a calamity. Their capture meant the substitution of one enslavement by a more severe one. Therefore, these Negroes must have been bitter anti-Indian propagandists among the slaves of South Carolina.

After the mid-century, Indians began stealing and selling more and more Negroes. In these years, White settlers increasingly encroached on Indian lands, coming in from almost all sides, and Indians struck back. These years were years of almost continuous warfare between Indians and Whites. Indians made a point of taking Negro slaves from these settlers to discourage their rush into the interior. It was also a fairly easy matter to steal Negroes from slaveholders in transit and in newly established settlements. Moreover, the American Revolution brought a new lawlessness to the South that lasted throughout the century. This meant that more Whites engaged in this Negro trade: these Whites encouraged Indians to steal Negroes and even stole Negroes themselves and disposed of them in the Indian country. British officers during the Revolution had a big part in promoting this Negro stealing: they got Indians, who sided with the British cause, to rob rebel slaveholders. After the Revolution, many White outlaws who were involved in this trade were British sympathizers. In time, this trade became well organized. Negroes were stolen from one part of the Indian frontier and carried into the Indian country and there traded about among Indians, and between Indians and Whites, until they ended up in slavery on another part of the Indian frontier.

Indians had little trouble selling these Negroes. Whites in the frontier settlements never had enough slaves. Moreover, law enforcement was lax. Sometimes Indians sold nearly every Negro they had. In 1784, Alexander McGillivray, the famous half-breed chief, reported that the Creeks were "now pretty well drained of Negroes." This trade extended outside the South. The Cherokee sold Negroes north of the Ohio River and Shawnee traders came from the North into the Creek country to buy Negroes. This trade even extended into the West Indies. In 1783, McGillivray sent Negroes to Pensacola for shipment to Jamaica. It is clear that Indians were avid and heartless slave traders. They looked upon these Negroes as nothing but chattel property. In 1796, John Sevier, Governor of Tennessee and slaveholder, reprimanded the Cherokee for trading Negroes to the Chickasaw for horses: he told them that "you know it is wrong to swop people for horses, for negroes is not horses tho they are black." These were the people Foster and Johnston have made out to be friends of Negroes. We can be sure that eighteenth century Negroes felt differently. We can not say, however, that Whites deliberately fostered this slave trade to create antagonism against Indians. But we can be sure that Whites did not fail to remind Negroes that Indians were slave traders.

Finally, Whites employed Indians to help crush slave insurrections. In the Stono Rebellion of 1739, the most serious insurrection in South Carolina during the eighteenth century, about eighty Negro slaves killed more than thirty Whites. At the outset, the Charles Town government called upon Settlement Indians for help. These Indians pursued those slaves who eluded the militia at Stono; in a few weeks, they managed to capture some of these slaves and to kill a few others. Indians also aided the province in suppressing slave insurrections in 1744 and 1765. Slave insurrections in the eighteenth century were small-scale affairs; South Carolinians did not need many Indians to help them restore order in any particular one. What mattered most was speed in putting them down; otherwise, more timid Negroes might respond to the call of liberty and join the rebel slaves. Therefore, for this job, the Charles Town government turned to Settlement Indians and Eastern Siouans. Although few in numbers, these Indians lived closer to White settlements and could be quickly mustered whenever needed.

The Charles Town government paid Indians high wages for helping suppress slave insurrections. In the Stono Rebellion, each Indian was given a coat, a flap, a pair of stockings, a hat, a gun, two pounds of powder, and eight pounds of bullets. The legislature, dominated by large slaveholders whose eyes were on the future, wanted to increase this payment. It declared that "Indians should be encouraged in such manner as to induce them always to offer their Service whenever this Government may have Occasion for them." In 1744, the Natchez, now living as scattered Settlement Indians in South Carolina after their defeat by the French in 1729, informed Governor Glen that they wanted to be "together to be ready to assist the Government in case of any Insurrection, or Rebellion of the Negroes." We can be certain that Negroes knew how eager Indians were to help keep them in slavery.

The Charles Town government did not wait for an uprising before calling on Indians. This government tried to anticipate trouble and then prevent it by using Indians to intimidate Negroes. On November 10, 1739, less than two months after Stono, the legislature ordered its Committee on Indian Affairs to cooperate with its special committee investigating this insurrection in "finding the most effectual means for preventing of such Dangers throughout the province." South Carolinians feared insurrections especially at Christmas, Negroes having so much more free time during these holidays. During the Christmas of 1716, the Charles Town government ordered Settlement Indians to move nearer White settlements to terrorize the slaves. Moreover, the government made a practice of locating Settlement Indians near places at which slaves might become troublesome. In the summer of 1716, it maintained the Wineau Indians around the Santee settlements "for keeping ye Negroes in awe." But South Carolinians did not rely only on Settlement Indians to prevent insurrections. These tribes and even the Catawba were not large enough to intimidate all Negroes in the province; there were not enough Settlement Indians to station at every danger point. As we know, South Carolinians saw the danger of a big insurrection in every little one. For intimidating all slaves, South Carolina needed at least one big inland tribe. Therefore, the government turned to its most trusted ally and probably the tribe most hostile to Negroes: the Cherokee. In 1737, Lieutenant-Governor Thomas Broughton reported that he was sending for Cherokee warriors "to come down to the settlements to be an awe to the negroes." Thus, a special effort was made after the Yamassee War to keep Negroes isolated from the Cherokee. In

1741, the legislature requested that Broughton purchase two Negro slaves owned by a Cherokee chief so that they could be shipped to the "West Indies or Northern Colonies to prevent any Detriment that they might do this Province by getting acquainted with the Cherokees." It is clear that this intimidation by Indians helped prevent slave insurrections.

CONCLUSIONS

Hostility between Indians and Negroes in the Colonial Southeast was more pronounced than friendliness. Southern Whites were afraid of these two colored races, each of which outnumbered them. Whites were especially afraid that these two exploited races would combine against them. To prevent this combination, Whites deliberately maintained social distance between Indians and Negroes and created antagonism between them. To maintain this social distance, Whites segregated Indians and Negroes from each other. They did this by keeping Indians out of White settlements as much as possible and by trying to keep Negroes out of the Indian country and other out of the way places where these colored races might meet. To create antagonism, Whites deliberately played Indians and Negroes against each other. They pointed out to these races that each was the enemy of the other. To this end of mutual hostility, Whites also used Negroes as soldiers against Indians; on the other hand, they used Indians to catch runaway slaves and to suppress slave insurrections. In the eyes of Negroes, Indians were enemies of Negro freedom. At times, Whites encouraged Indians and Negroes to murder each other. In these ways, Whites created much of the hostility between Indians and Negroes in the eighteenth century.

Slavery

DAVID BRION DAVIS

• The institution of slavery started in the British colonies as an attempt to cope with severe labor shortages. The first boatload of Africans arrived in 1619, and for the next forty years the blacks were sometimes treated as indentured servants—workers who toiled for a fixed period of time and then freed to pursue their own lives—and sometimes kept forever in bondage. Not until the 1660's did the custom develop to keep all Afro-Americans in permanent servitude. Thereafter the African slaves provided the bulk of the laboring force in the southern colonies. Slavery existed in the North also during this period, but it was not widespread. The institution was generally curbed, and the bondsmen released before the Civil War. In the South the invention of the cotton gin in 1793 created an enormous need for slaves to support an essentially agricultural economy.

In the following essay David Brion Davis compares slavery in the British colonies and the United States with its counterparts in other societies. Although he finds numerous specific differences, he argues that the conditions of slaves were relatively similar from culture to culture. One of Davis's most provocative statements is that "prejudice against Negroes seems to have grown in the United States with the advance of popular democracy." Is our society really one where advances for some people can be made only by suppression of others?

From *The Comparative Approach to American History*, edited by C. Vann Woodward. Copyright © 1968 by C. Vann Woodward. Reprinted by permission of Basic Books, Inc., Publishers, New York.

Of all American institutions, Negro slavery has probably been the one most frequently compared with historical antecedents and foreign counterparts, and with the least benefit to systematic knowledge. Quite understandably, modern scholars have been so impressed by the long submission and degradation of southern Negroes, as well as by the extraordinary prevalence of racial prejudice in the United States, that they have often pictured American slavery as a system of unique and unmitigated severity that stands in marked contrast to other forms of servitude. Yet Thomas Jefferson could confidently assert that in Augustan Rome the condition of slaves was "much more deplorable than that of the blacks on the continent of America," and list barbarities and cruelties which were commonplace in Rome but presumably unknown in Virginia. Apologists for American slavery were always fond of comparing the mildness of their own institution, supposedly evidenced by a rapidly increasing Negro population, with the harshness of slavery in the West Indies or ancient Rome, where a constant supply of fresh captives made up for an appalling mortality. Yet abolitionists were always inclined to argue that the slave system of their own country or empire was the worst in history. Foreign travelers were not only subject to nationalistic prejudice but tended to rank various slave systems on the basis of fortuitous impressions or the biased accounts of hospitable planters. When we recognize how often comparisons have been influenced by ulterior motives and have been directed to the fruitless question "Which nation's slavery was the worst?" we might conclude that the subject can most profitably be studied in geographical isolation.

Yet American slavery was a product of the African slave trade, which was itself an integral part of both European commercial expansion and New World colonization. Most of the components of the slave-trading and plantation systems were developed in the thirteenth and fourteenth centuries by Italian merchants who purchased Circassians, Tartars, and Georgians at commercial bases on the Black Sea and then transported them to markets in Egypt, Italy, and Spain. As early as 1300 the enterprising Italians were even working Negro slaves on sugar plantations in Cyprus. In the fifteenth century, when the Portuguese adopted similar practices in trading with West Africa, Negro slaves displaced the Moors and Russians as the lowest element in the labor force of Spain. Negroes were shipped to Hispaniola as early as 1502; and as the Spanish colonists gradually turned to the cultivation of sugar, the rising demand for labor became an enormous stimulus to the Portuguese African trade. By the seventeenth century the Atlantic slave trade had become a vast international enterprise as the Dutch, British, French, Danes, Swedes, and even Brandenburgers established forts and markets along the West African coast. On both sides of the Atlantic there was close contact between merchants, seamen, and planters of various nationalities. In addition to competing and fighting with one another, they borrowed techniques and customs, cooperated in smuggling, and gathered to buy slaves at such entrepôts as Curaçao. If the British planters of Barbados looked to Brazil as a model, Barbados itself provided the impulse for settling Carolina. There was, then, a high degree of institutional continuity which linked the European maritime powers in a common venture. A trade which involved six major nations and lasted for three centuries, which transported some 10 to 15 million Africans to the New World, and which became a central part of international rivalry and the struggle for empire, cannot be considered as a mere chapter in the history of North America.

The unpleasant truth is that there could hardly have been successful colonization of the New World without Negro slaves, since there was no alternative source of labor to meet the needs required by the cultivation of sugar, rice, tobacco, and cotton, and since even the more diversified colonies were long dependent economically on the markets and earnings of the staple-producing regions. It must be emphasized that this common dependence on Negro slavery was never universally recognized or welcomed. From the first Spanish in Hispaniola to the British in Barbados and Virginia, colonists were slow and hesitant in committing themselves to a labor force of foreign captives. Among the frequent dreams of New World Utopias and second Edens, no one envisioned a model society of several thousand free Europeans overseeing the life and labor of several hundred thousand Negro slaves. From the beginning, racial antipathy was reinforced by the much stronger emotion of fear; and the dread of insurrection and racial war would always balance the desire for quick wealth through a reckless increase in slaves.

Nonetheless, from sixteenth-century Mexico to eighteenth-century Jamaica and South Carolina, colonial administrators were unable to maintain a reassuring ratio between white immigrants and Negro slaves. In regions where tropical or semitropical staples could be cultivated, it became clear that investment in slave labor was the key to expanded production and spectacular profit. The Negro slave played an indispensable role in the conquest and settlement of Latin America, and in the clearing and cultivation of virgin land from Trinidad to the lower Mississippi Valley and Texas. And as the possession of slaves became itself a symbol of affluence, prestige, and power, the demand for Negroes spread to urban and temperate zones. Important leaders in New England and French Canada seriously argued that only Negro slaves could meet the labor needs of their colonies. From 1732 to 1754 Negro slaves constituted more than 35 per cent of the immigrants entering New York City; by mid-century they were owned by about one-tenth of the householders of the province and accounted for 15 per cent of the total population. Meanwhile, the slave trade and American Negro slavery were sanctioned by treaties and the law of nations, by the acts and edicts of kings and parliaments, by the Spanish Council of the Indies and the great trading companies of England, Holland, and France, by the Catholic Church and the major Protestant denominations. All the colonies of the New World legalized the institution, and many competed with one another for a supply of labor that was never equal to the demand. For more than three centuries the Negro slave was deeply involved in imperial wars, revolutions, and wars of independence. Insofar as the Western Hemisphere has a common history, it must center on a common experience with Negro slavery.

But did slavery mean the same thing to the various colonists of the New World? The fact that Dutch slave traders imitated the Portuguese and that a Dutch ship brought the first Negroes to Virginia did not mean that a Negro's status would be the same in Virginia as in Brazil. In England, unlike Italy and the Iberian Peninsula, true slavery disappeared by the thirteenth century. On the other hand, English jurists perpetuated the legal concept of unlimited servitude, and English judges recognized the validity of enslaving and selling infidels. We still have much to learn about the character of servitude in the sixteenth century and the later evolution of slave status in the British, Dutch, and French colonies. In making future comparative studies it would be well to keep in mind two points which should prevent hasty generalizations. First, in many societies the slave has only gradually been differentiated from other kinds of unfree workers, and his status, rights, and obligations have been defined in practice before receiving legal recognition. Second, although the actual condition of slaves has varied greatly even within a single society, there has been a remarkable persistence and uniformity in the legal concept of the slave. Since this last point has often been disregarded in comparative approaches to American slavery, we shall elaborate on it here.

The status of slavery has always been surrounded with certain ambiguities that seem related to the institution's origins. To be enslaved as a result of capture in war or punishment for crime implied total subordination to coercive authority. Yet bondage for debt or as the result of self-sale suggested merely a reciprocal exchange of labor and obedience for sustenance and protection. When a bondwoman's offspring were claimed by her owner on the same basis as the natural increase of livestock, the status was assimilated to that of movable property. In societies where slaves have largely been recruited from the native poor and have performed no specialized economic function, as in ancient China, Egypt, and the Near East, the element of reciprocal rights and obligations has taken precedence over the elements of punishment and ownership. Nevertheless, the slave was legally defined as a thing not only in the Southern United States but in ancient Egypt, Babylonia, Greece, and Rome. And the Roman conception of the slave as at once a person and a piece of movable property prevailed in medieval France, Italy, and Spain; it was extended to Latin America and was incorporated in the Code Noir for the French colonies; and it reappeared in the laws and judicial decisions of British North America. A Virginia court merely affirmed the ancient Latin concept of chattel slavery when it ruled that "Slaves are not only property, but they are rational beings, and entitled to the humanity of the Court, when it can be exercised without invading the rights of property." And when an American master claimed the offspring of his female slaves or asserted his right to move, sell, trade, bequest, or give away his chattel property, he added nothing to a legal notion of slavery that had persisted in Europe for more than two thousand years.

The definition of the slave as chattel property implied a condition of rightlessness on the part of the slave. In neither Europe nor the

Americas could a slave testify in court against a free person, institute a court action in his own behalf, make a legally binding will or contract, or own property. There were, to be sure, minor exceptions and variations. Slaves were sometimes allowed to testify in certain civil cases or give evidence against a master accused of treason. In North America at various times Negro bondsmen were permitted to plead benefit of clergy and to give evidence in capital cases involving other slaves. As in Rome and Latin America, they were accorded limited rights over personal property, including horses and cattle, and might act as a master's legal agent, though never with the freedom and complex prerogatives of the Roman slave. But what stands out above the exceptions and variations is the fact that from pre-Christian laws to the slave codes of the New World the bondsman had no civil capacities and was considered only as an extension of his master's legal personality. Even in Puritan Massachusetts slaves were, in the words of Cotton Mather, who was simply echoing Aristotle, "the *Animate, Separate, Active Instruments* of other men."

One of the few significant differences in the legal status of slaves was that bondsmen were denied legal marriage in ancient Rome and in Protestant America, whereas slave marriages were recognized in Carthage, Hellenistic Greece, and in Catholic Europe and America. Largely to prevent the sin of fornication, Catholic theologians even ruled that a slave might marry against his master's will. Yet according to St. Thomas Aquinas, slavery was an "impediment" to marriage, comparable to impotence, and a slave's first obligation must be to his master, not his spouse. If a master had a moral duty to try to preserve the integrity of slave families, he still had a legal claim to all slave children, and might of necessity divide husband from wife or children from parents. Since there is evidence that Latin American masters often did little to encourage or respect slave marriages, and that North American masters often recognized such marriages and tried to keep families intact, one may suspect that actual differences were more the result of individual personality and economic pressure than of legal and moral rights. The main point is that in no society have slaves had a legal claim to their wives and children.

Religious conversion has always complicated the question of a slave's status. The Muslims and ancient Hebrews drew a sharp distinction between enslaving infidels and temporarily holding servants of their own faith who had been deprived of freedom by economic necessity. Although the first Church Fathers ruled unmistakably that baptism should have no effect on the temporal status of slaves, medieval Christians showed an increasing reluctance to enslave their fellow Christians and came to think of perpetual bondage as a punishment suitable only for infidels. But the authorities who condemned the sale of Christians and yet preached slaving crusades against the infidels were ultimately faced with the problem of the baptized infidel. In 1366 the priors of Florence explained that it was valid to buy or sell slaves who had been baptized so long as they had originally come "from the land and race of the infidels." This was, in effect, the same test later applied in Virginia and other North American colonies. Baptism was to have no effect on a slave's status unless he had been a Christian in his native country. And if the Catholic colonists felt a much greater obligation to have their slaves baptized, North American laws encouraged conversion and recognized that the Negro had a soul that might be redeemed. After a century of inaction, the Protestant churches slowly began their work of spreading religion among the slaves, and by the mid-nineteenth century the proportion of converted Negroes was probably as large in parts of the United States as in Brazil. It is doubtful, however, whether the mass of slaves in any country ever enjoyed a meaningful religious life.

There was little that was distinctive in the police regulations and penal laws restricting the lives of North American slaves. Throughout the ages, and in virtually all parts of the Western Hemisphere, slaves were prohibited from carrying arms, traveling at night or without permission, and acting with disrespect toward a freeman. Fairly typical was a law of 1785 for Spanish Santo Domingo which ordered one hundred lashes and two years in jail for any Negro who raised his hand against a white man. The penalties for such crimes as theft and assault were everywhere more severe for slaves than for others. During the eighteenth century there was a tendency in most New World colonies to abandon the most sanguinary punishments, such as mutilation, dismemberment, and burning at the stake. Harsh restrictions and terrifying punishments persisted longest in the West Indies, where the disproportion of Negroes to whites was the greatest. But even in the West Indies the long-term trend was toward more humane punishment and an extension of the slave's legal protections.

It is misleading to say that Anglo-American law never recognized the Negro slave as a human personality whose rights to life, food, and shelter were protected by law. There was ample precedent for the 1846 ruling of a Kentucky judge that "A slave is not in the condition of a horse. . . . He is made after the image of the Creator. He has mental capacities, and an immortal principle in his nature. . . . The law . . . cannot extinguish his high born nature, nor deprive him of many rights which are inherent in man." Although a master might kill his slave with impunity in the ancient Near East, the Roman Republic, Saxon England, and under certain circumstances in the Iberian Peninsula and Latin America, and although in much of British America the murder of a slave was thought to merit only a modest fine, by the early nineteenth century the slave states of North America had put the killing or maiming of a Negro bondsman on the same level of criminality as the killing or maiming of a white man. In both the British Caribbean and the Southern states, courts sometimes held that slaves were protected by common law against such crimes as manslaughter or unprovoked battery. Georgia and North Carolina both held that slaves had a right to trial by jury, and North Carolina went so far as to recognize a slave's right to resist unprovoked attack. Of course it was one thing for American states to threaten punishment for cruelty to slaves, and to make masters legally obligated to give their bondsmen adequate food and shelter and to provide for their care in sickness and old age, and it was another matter to enforce such laws when Negroes were barred from testifying against white men. Nevertheless, one can plausibly argue that in terms of legal protections and physical welfare American slaves by the 1850's were as favorably treated as any bondsmen in history.

Yet one of the paradoxes of American slavery was that the laws protecting the physical welfare of slaves were accompanied by the severest restrictions on manumission. This brings us to the most important distinction between the legal status of slaves in British and Latin America. It should be stressed that taxes and other restrictions on manumission were common in antiquity, particularly in Rome, and that freedom suffered from prejudice and legal disabilities even when the stigma of slavish origin was not associated with race. There were discriminatory freedmen's laws, for example, in medieval Spain and Italy, and in Latin America as well. But only in the Southern

United States did legislators try to bar every route to emancipation and deprive masters of their traditional right to free individual slaves. It is true that thousands of American slaves were manumitted by their owners, many after buying their freedom in installments, as was far more common in Latin America. It is also true that in some areas of Latin America a slave had no more realistic chance of becoming free than did his brother in Mississippi. Nevertheless, one may conclude that slavery in North America was distinctive in its efforts to build ever higher barriers against manumission. And there is evidence that this had less to do with slavery as such than with social attitudes toward racial integration.

Although the questions are of compelling importance, we cannot begin to determine whether slavery was a source of racial prejudice or prejudice a source of slavery, nor can we explain why prejudice became more dominant in the United States than in other parts of the New World. One may briefly state the principal facts that are relevant to a comparative study of slavery. Without denying the significance of racial difference as an aggravation to American bondage, we may note that throughout history slaves have been said to be naturally inferior, lazy, cunning, thievish, lascivious, fawning, deceitful, and incapable of life's higher thoughts and emotions. When not differentiated by race, they have often been physically marked off by shaven heads, brands, tattoos, and collars. There is unmistakable evidence of racial prejudice in Italy and the Iberian Peninsula, where colored slaves generally suffered from various indignities and disabilities. In Latin America Negro bondsmen were long denied the privileges and protections of Indian workers. Nonetheless, while Latin America was by no means immune from racial prejudice, even against freemen of mixed blood, there was a gradual acceptance of racial intermixture and a willingness to accept each stage of dilution as a step toward whiteness. In the British colonies, although the first Negroes had an ill-defined status and worked side by side with white servants, there was never any tolerance of racial blending. White fathers seldom acknowledged their colored offspring, and a mulatto or quadroon was still legally classed as a Negro. These differences may have been related to religion, sexual mores, social stratification, or the proportion of white women in a colonial population. But whatever the reason, prejudice against Negroes seems to have grown in the United States with the advance of popular democracy. It can be argued that this had less to do with slavery than with the status of the free Negro in an unusually mobile and unstratified white society. In other words, differences in slave systems may not account for the fact that while the Negro in the United States today has far more economic and educational opportunities than the Negro in Latin America, he also suffers from more overt discrimination from whites who feel superior but are unsure of their own status.

By focusing thus far on the legal status of slaves, we have given an oversimplified picture of institutional homogeneity. In actuality, of course, American slavery took a great variety of forms that were largely the result of economic pressures and such derivative factors as the nature of employment, the number of slaves owned by a a typical master, and the proportion of slaves in a given society. Thus we correctly categorize North American slavery as plantation and staple-crop slavery, but tend to forget that in 1820 Negro bondsmen constituted 20 per cent of the population of Southern cities and that in 1860 there were a half million slaves working in factories, on railroad construction, as stevedores, as lumberjacks, on steamboats, and in numerous other jobs unconnected with agriculture. As in ancient Athens and Rome, and as in Latin America, slaves in the Southern states were employed as valets, waiters, cooks, nurses, craftsmen, and prostitutes. In spite of these well-known facts, most comparisons of slavery in British and Latin America have assumed that the institutions were virtually monolithic. We still lack comparative studies of the domestic servant, the slave artisan, the rented worker, and the slave in manufacturing establishments.

It has been said that the latifundia of southern Italy and Sicily provided an ancient precedent for the gang labor, the rationalized system of production, and the absentee ownership of the Caribbean plantation. But one must be careful not to lump all plantation agriculture in an undifferentiated class. Since the production of sugar, for example, was a long and continuous process that could be ruined by a delay in cutting, milling, boiling, or curing, the rhythm of plantation life was probably much the same in parts of Brazil as in Jamaica and Louisiana. The cultivation of sugar and rice required heavy capital investment, and in the West Indies and South Carolina led to slave gangs of several hundred being divided for specialized tasks under constant surveillance. Slavery in colonial South Carolina, though less characterized by absentee ownership, had more in common with slavery in the West Indies than either had with the institution in Virginia and Maryland. By 1765 South Carolina's forty thousand whites were outnumbered by ninety thousand slaves; eight years later Jamaica's sixteen thousand whites kept uneasy watch over two hundred thousand slaves. In neither society could a field slave be in close or frequent contact with white men. In Virginia, on the other hand, the proportion of Negroes and whites was roughly equal, and the typical tobacco plantation employed less than twenty slaves. Unlike any of the previously mentioned staples, cotton did not require elaborate stages of preparation and processing, and could be profitably grown on small-scale farms. It was thus not uncommon for a cotton farmer to own less than ten slaves and even to work beside them in the field. Even by 1860, after a long period of rising slave prices, nearly one-half of the Southern slaveholders owned less than five Negroes apiece; 72 per cent owned less than ten apiece and held approximately one-quarter of the entire number of American slaves.

Compared with the plantation agriculture of the West Indies and Brazil, the striking features of the American South were the wide dispersal of slave ownership and the relatively small units of production scattered over immense areas. This may have led to a greater variation and flexibility in the relationship between master and slaves, although we still lack comparative research on such vital questions as labor management, the social roles and subculture of Negroes, and the relation of plantation life to social structure. It seems plausible that if American Negroes sometimes benefited by a close relationship with white families, they were also denied the sense of massive solidarity that was probably essential for revolt. In the West Indies slaves not only had the opportunity to plan and organize revolts, but they were seldom tied by the close bonds of loyalty that led so many North American slaves to divulge plots before they were hardly formed.

This is not to suggest that North American slaves were less oppressed than those of other times and regions, but only that there were different forms of oppression. As comparative studies move ahead toward finer distinctions and a typology of slave systems, it is likely that less attention will be paid to legal status than to stages of economic development. It would be absurd to claim that all slave economies must pass through a pre-set cycle of boom and depression. Nevertheless, regardless of cultural differences and other variables, there are striking examples throughout the Americas of a pattern which began with an unmitigated drive for quick profit, a rapid expansion in slaves and land under cultivation, and a subsequent overproduction of staples. Whenever slaves were worked under boom conditions, as in the West Indies in the mid-eighteenth century and the Brazilian coffee plantations in the nineteenth, the institution was one of grinding attrition. A more relaxed paternalism tended to appear when prices had fallen, when there was little incentive to maximize production, and when planters in longer-settled regions looked to social and cultural distinctions to differentiate themselves from new generations of hard-driving speculators. Thus in the mid-nineteenth century there is evidence that in such states as Virginia and Maryland a more easy-going, paternalistic pattern of slavery was emerging, not unlike that of the depleted sugar plantations of Brazil. In Maryland and Delaware there was even a rapid decline in the proportion of slaves to freedmen, though this was partly a result of interstate migration. At the same time there was a heavy drain of slaves toward the expanding cotton areas of the Southwest, where the price of labor kept rising and slaves became more concentrated in the hands of a relatively few planters.

The question of stages of economic development is related to the much larger question of the place of slavery in the evolution of industrial capitalism. And here, though historians have long acknowledged the dependence of the world's cotton textile industry on the slave systems of North and South America, there is an astonishing lack of systematic and comparative analysis. The whole complex relationship between capitalism and slavery is still in the realm of suggestive speculation. Scholars still debate whether slavery was profitable and whether the forms it took in America can be termed capitalistic. We do not yet fully understand why so many areas where slavery flourished were stultified by soil depletion and a lack of capital formation, by an absence of internal markets, of urbanization, and of technological innovation. And finally, if we are really to comprehend the significance of slavery and the burdens it has entailed, comparative history must explain the great challenge posed to the institution by an emerging urban, bureaucratic, and capitalistic civilization, which led to a bitter conflict between England and her Caribbean colonies, to a sharp struggle between the Brazilian coastal cities and the interior valleys, and to an epic contest between the North and South in the United States.

The American Revolution: Was It a Real One?

DAVID HAWKE

• Whether used by students or statesmen the word "revolution" arouses misgivings and even terror in the majority of the American people. Perhaps this is due to the normal human preference for the comfort of the tried and the true rather than the uncertainty of a new situation. The idea of revolution was also disturbing to our colonial forefathers. A large portion of the citizenry, including Benjamin Franklin, hoped for some kind of settlement, short of an open break, of their quarrel with the mother country. This is contrary to the popular stereotype of a people united from the beginning in a desire for independence from England and imbued with the vision of a continental destiny.

In the following article, David Hawke maintains that the seeds of the revolution were planted by a group of bright, talented, and educated young men whose thoughts were of individual dreams and destinies. To them, the British Empire was a frustrating roadblock in their drive for personal advancement and recognition. But they were not merely opportunistic rebels; they believed in John Locke's notion of natural right, they believed that just governments rested upon the consent of the governed, they believed in the American dream. And the political upheaval they spawned brought social changes as well. As Professor Hawke examines the position and ideology of the young men whose determination led to the first major revolution of modern times, consider the validity of the author's interpretation. Could a man as successful as George Washington actually feel frustrated?

From *Pace*, published by Pace College, Vol. 17, No. 3 (August 1966). Reprinted by permission.

Our leaders of today find it hard sometimes to face up to our revolutionary past. Indeed, the word "revolution" has become almost a subversive word, one that belongs to the Communists rather than to Americans. No longer do we urge subjugated people to emulate our spirit of '76 and rebel against their oppressors. Instead, the United States encourages the oppressed throughout the world to reject revolt as a solution to their ills. Be patient, we say, let the United States help, and in time the good society will come about without bloodshed. The CIA may take a different tack, but then the CIA after all is regarded by some as an un-American outfit.

This general uneasiness about our past led some people long ago to rename the American Revolution the War for Independence. This is a soothing notion. It gets the State Department out of a sticky situation. It calms those of conservative leanings who might be distressed to think that the United States, like modern Russia, was born a child of revolution. The Sons and Daughters of the American Revolution rest easier, and the John Birch Society, of course, is immensely relieved.

Competent historians have done much to promote the view that the spirit of '76 was a conservative movement led by dignified gentlemen eager only to preserve customs, habits, and institutions that Great Britain seemed determined to trample under. They have shown, quite convincingly, that there was no sign of a class uprising in 1776; that the American people in the 18th century were the most prosperous, the most comfortable, the lowest-taxed citizens in the world; that their complaints against Great Britain, relative to the ills of European people, were minor; and that at most they sought only independence from Britain.

These historians who reject the idea of revolution do not go so far as to see no basic changes coming out of the War for Independence. One change that occurred was so fundamental that all must admit it was revolutionary. Prior to the war the drink that nourished the soul and promoted good talk throughout America was rum. But the war cut contacts with the West Indian islands that produced the sugar and molasses from which the rum was made. The result was, as a charmed Spanish visitor noted, that the ingenious Americans "distilled the juice of cornstalks and from this made whisky."

But if we put aside the contribution of bourbon to the American spirit and diet, it is clear a strong case can be made that socially, politically, and otherwise little occurred to distinguish post-war America from pre-war America except that independence had been declared. Nonetheless, I contend that the war was a product of a desire much deeper and stronger than independence, that it was, indeed, as much a revolution as any that has occurred in history—revolutionary in the impulse that drove the leaders, in the principles that guided their actions, in the techniques they used, and in the achievements that ultimately came forth.

First, let's look at the impulse of the men behind the Revolution. It is true that no evidence has been found to show that the mass of people was especially disturbed or eager to rise up and take control of their colonial governments prior to the Revolution. Indeed, the most notable fact is their political apathy. They had to be constantly prodded to vote. They seemed content to plow their fields or tend their shops and leave politics up to a few gentlemen interested in that art.

But to say that the common people were content is not to say there was no unrest in America. There was, I suggest, much unrest—not at the bottom, nor at the top, but in the upper level of what I suppose must be called the great middle class.

It is difficult for us today to see George Washington, Thomas Jefferson, or Benjamin Rush—to name only three—as men with anything in common with the seedy characters who have fomented revolutions in other nations. Were they not of the elite men respected for their education, intelligence, welcomed and admired wherever they went? Had not each of these three men—one a soldier, one a lawyer-politician, and one a physician—acquired distinction in his profession? How is it possible to say they were so dissatisfied they were willing to lead a revolution?

Let's look at Thomas Jefferson, a most sedate and cautious gentleman, born to wealth and patient enough to wait to fall in love with a rich widow who brought even more wealth to the marriage. At no time was Jefferson frustrated by failure. At the age of 26, he had won the highest elective office in his colony—a seat in the House of Burgesses. What lay ahead for him "on the road to glory," to use a phrase he liked? Little. He could advance to important committees in the House but never to real power. At 26 the door to advancement for this man of powerful mind, of great and restless energy had been closed.

Let us look at George Washington. At 22, he had the dubious honor of starting a world war. The fracas he initiated in the forests of Pennsylvania in 1754 launched the French and Indian War which two years later enlarged into the Seven Years' War, engaging the energies of all Europe's major powers. Four years later Washington reached the peak of his career, or so it seemed, when he commanded two divisions under General Forbes on the expedition to take Fort Duquesne. After that he resigned from the service. It must have been clear to him at the age of 26, he had gone as far as he could go, that as long as the British army ran military affairs in America he would never rise above the rank of colonel. He was destined, in effect, always to be a bridesmaid, never a bride.

Let us, finally, look at Benjamin Rush, who when he died early in the 19th century was considered the most eminent physician in all the United States. Rush returned home to Philadelphia in 1769 after two years of study at Edinburgh and London and equipped with what was then regarded as the best possible medical education available in the world. Rush was a great complainer all his life. He was of the sort who saw a meteor in the sky and became convinced at once it was aimed at him and him alone. For all that, it is clear that Rush quickly became convinced after his return to Philadelphia that his career as a physician was blocked by a right little band of elite at the top of Philadelphia society. His letters reveal a constant sense of frustration, of being blocked in his advancement.

These three gentlemen and hundreds of others scattered through the colonies must have sensed in the 1770's that despite their intelligence and their training, their careers could advance so far and then no further unless they became part of the Establishment.

The problem was that America in the 18th century was a provincial society. Its culture, for all its Americanization, was still essentially English. The books Americans read, the clothes they wore, the furnishings of their homes all came from England or were patterned on English designs. Being reared in a provincial culture is tolerable if there is a possibility of escape—if there is a reasonable chance of settling in at the center of power. Bright young men from Liverpool, Edinburgh, Manchester, and York could with relative ease pull up stakes and travel down to London for fame and fortune. London was filled with provincials—Boswell from Edinburgh, Sam Johnson from Litchfield, William and John Hunter, the city's two most eminent surgeons who both came from a Scots village.

But this outlet was available to few Americans and appealed to even fewer. Benjamin West, John Singleton Copley, and to a degree Benjamin Franklin availed themselves of it, but most Americans found this escape hatch unattractive. True, Rush momentarily thought of returning to London in 1771 to make his reputation but was discouraged by a physician who had been his mentor there.

It seems to be impossible to exaggerate the sense of frustration the bright, talented, and educated in colonial America felt in the 1760's and 1770's, the anger that rose up within their breasts when they saw that they could advance only so far and that unless, through political pull or family connection, they could work into the Establishment, they were blocked forever.

These men, who were to become the founding fathers of the republic, may appear safe and sedate to us today—as a matter of fact, I am afraid that we historians have to take some of the blame for having sanitized them. They were not, however, any different, it seems to me, in their attitude toward what they wanted to achieve—their sense of frustration—than the people who were leaders of the Puritan Revolution of 17th century England or the French Revolution in 18th century France. Their writings, for example, are as vituperative, audacious, and filled with lament about the end of civilization unless some change comes—a feeling that the world must be changed completely by a revolution in America. You only have to read some of the contemporary works of Rush, who saw the revolution as a chance to reform all of American society, or of Thomas Jefferson, who saw the king and all of the king's minions as the most corrupt influence that America ever endured, to understand how revolutionary these men were in their thought. They expressed themselves, in other words, in their writing with as much vituperation against the Crown, with as much desire to reform the world as anybody in any Communist, Chinese, English or French revolution.

So much for the impulse of these men. Let's turn now to a second point. I hold that it was not only a revolution in the sense that the leaders were driven by an impulse to revolt, but it was also a revolution based on principles, not just for independence, but for much more.

Year ago it was held that Americans blundered their way toward a rationale for independence, that they were pushed by events to take stands rather than reacting to events evolved out of a set of fixed principles. Professor Edmund Morgan recently developed a thesis, now generally accepted by historians, that in 1765, at the time of the Stamp Act, the colonists took a stand on a constitutional principle from which they never deviated. They held that Parliament had no right to legislate any taxes—internal or external—on the colonies. From that initial stand came all the principles on which the Americans justified their break with Great Britain. During the decade following the Stamp Act, a small flood of pamphlets flowed from American printing presses. Each of these refined, clarified, or elaborated the initial stand into a full set of political principles. By the end of the decade a consensus had been reached throughout the colonies as to exactly what the Americans stood for. First, it was agreed that just governments were those which were based on the consent of the governed. The people were sovereign. Second, these governments had been made through covenants between the rulers and the ruled. Third, that the people had certain inalienable rights, among which were the rights to life, liberty, and property, and it was the duty of the government to protect these rights. Fourth, Americans were members of the British empire but their only tie was through the Crown, not with Parliament. As long as the king minded his manners Americans enjoyed being members of the empire.

By the early 1770's a few bold spirits like John Adams, James Wilson, and Thomas Jefferson advanced the view that the Crown had broken its covenant with Americans. The monarchy and all that came with it had become corrupt. If the monarchy did not reform itself, there was nothing left for the American people to do but declare their independence.

Now, it was one thing to establish a set of revolutionary principles—or, rather, a set of principles on which to base a revolution. It was another matter to put those principles into action. In a country where the people showed little interest in imperial affairs or provincial politics something more than an appeal to reason was needed to persuade the people to act on these principles. This leads to my third point, that the thirteen colonies were carried toward independence by a variety of pressures. Among these, the British attacks on Lexington and Concord, on Norfolk, Virginia; on Falmouth, in Maine, and so forth, certainly did much to put the people in a revolutionary mood. But British activity at no time sufficed to make a majority of Americans in 1776 independent-minded. I tread on thin ground here, but I have never found anything to contradict John Adams' remark that during the Revolution one-third of the people were for it, one-third against, and one-third didn't care. The Revolution was, in short, a minority movement. Somehow the country had to be manipulated toward independence. It was clear, as one delegate in Congress remarked during the debate over independence, that if they waited for the people to lead the way independence would never be declared.

Propaganda, as in all revolutions, did much to promote the cause of independence. "It is our business to improve upon events," Sam Adams remarked at one point and he never ceased to follow his own advice. The most influential piece of propaganda was Paine's *Common Sense*. No other book, except *Uncle Tom's Cabin*, had such an effect on shaping American minds. But more than propaganda was needed.

One of the key persons who carried the country toward the break with Britain was George Washington. Americans have not liked to face the fact the military often exerts pressure on public opinion and only recently, through the research of Professor Curtis Nettels, has it become clear how much Washington used his army to promote independence wherever it needed promoting. For instance, he received a report that "that infernal crew of Tories" were making matters difficult for independent-minded men in New Hampshire. Washington told his man on the scene, General John Sullivan, to seize all officers of the Crown who were "acting as enemies of their country." This was the first official definition of Tories and the first directive ordering them to be seized. Washington's order coupled with the presence of Sullivan's troops hamstrung the king's friends in New Hampshire. The militant leaders there now dared to call a constitutional convention, and within a few months New Hampshire became the first colony ruled by a government that drew its authority from the people, not the king.

When Governor Trumbull of Connecticut wondered how to deal with the Tories in his midst, Washington helped to clarify his thoughts. "Why should persons who are preying upon the vitals of their country be suffered to stalk at large, whilst we know they will do us every mischief in their power!" he asked. Connecticut, knowing it would be backed by the army, became the first colony to produce a series of laws directed against the Tories. In a similar way Washington strengthened the resolve of Rhode Island leaders. The assembly passed acts in November defining treason, and the next month General Charles Lee toured the colony forcing an oath of loyalty on all suspected Tories.

In Pennsylvania the manipulation was undercover and carried out completely by independent-minded men. The people, in an election on May 1, 1776, had in effect chosen an assembly where the majority of members still wanted to plump for reconciliation with Britain. Without Pennsylvania independence could never be declared, for it was the richest of the colonies in men, natural resources, and trained craftsmen. A series of carefully arranged mass meetings, newspaper articles, propaganda directed at the young men who would be doing the fighting put the assembly in such a disreputable light that the mass meetings repudiated that body, called for a conference of delegates who would in turn lay the groundwork for a constitutional convention which would side-step the assembly. In the end, by the most nefarious techniques, in which both John and Sam Adams participated, the Pennsylvania assembly was overturned, a pro-independent delegation ended up in Congress and independence was soon after voted.

The Revolution did not achieve all that its leaders set out to achieve. For instance, many people were unhappy that at the end of the war they were still speaking English. The new nation needed a new language but what should it be? "Some people," a visiting Frenchman remarked, "for the convenience of the public, wanted Hebrew to take the place of English; it would have been taught in the schools, and made use of for all public documents. It may readily be imagined that this proposal had no sequel; but we may conclude from the mere suggestion that the Americans could not express in a more energetic manner their aversion for the English." Noah Webster decided Hebrew would be too much even for Americans, but he, too, was determined to make America "as independent and illustrious in letters as she is already in arms and civil policy," and to that end he worked to supplant the English with the American language. It is through Webster's doing that the "u" was dropped from such words as "labour" and "honour" and that such Anglicanisms as "gaol" became "jail."

The first and most revolutionary achievement was the establishment of republican governments. This, in a world of monarchies, was "an audacious and radical" experiment. The leaders knew the boldness of what they were doing and were proud of themselves. "It was reserved for Americans," one said in 1778, "to put government on its proper foundations, the sovereignty of the people." Second, in a world of unitary governments, the Americans dared to construct a confederated system, which they later modified into a federated system. Third, in a world ruled by fiat and custom, they dared to construct governments under plainly written constitutions.

How had they managed this? Partly because they had eliminated from the body politic virtually all among the elite who might have opposed these experiments—the loyalists, some 60,000 to 100,000 of the country's well-to-do. In the French Revolution, which no one doubts was a real revolution, there were five emigres per thousand people; in the American Revolution, there were twenty-four emigres per thousand. A majority of the French emigres eventually returned home after the war to revive the aristocratic order. Hardly any of those who left America returned after the war. "The sense in which there was no conflict in the American Revolution," says Robert Palmer, "is the sense in which the loyalists are forgotten."

These new republican governments fit the principles that American leaders had been developing the past decade, and that, too, made it easy to put them into operation.

Now to what extent were these new governments revolutionary, how much did they differ practically—not just theoretically—from what had gone before? Not as much as some of the leaders would have liked. For instance, Thomas Jefferson concluded that at least half the white male residents over twenty-one of Virginia lacked the right to vote because they lacked sufficient property. He wanted to extend "the right of suffrage (or in other words the rights of a citizen) to all who had a permanent intention of living in the country." "Whoever intends to live in a country must wish that country well, and has a natural right of assisting in the preservation of it." To that end, he called for lowering property qualifications for suffrage and for liberal land grants to all who lacked the requisite amounts of land. His idea got nowhere; the new Virginia constitution of 1776 called for no changes at all in voting requirements.

But there were fundamental changes nonetheless in all the state constitutions that came forth—some ten of them during 1776 and 1777, which has been called the most creative period of constitution-making in American history. The theory of checks and balances, for the most part, was shunted aside in all these constitutions. None provided for the legislative, judicial, and executive branches to check and balance one another. The lower house in nearly all dominated the government, choosing the governor, appointing the judiciary, controlling the finances. The Governor lost his veto over state legislation in every state but New York and even there he could be overridden by the legislature. He was chosen by the legislators in all states but New York. Pennsylvania went so far as to eliminate the Governor's post and substitute a committee to run state affairs. The men who made the new constitutions were so certain their work was perfect that only one constitution provided for amendments.

Despite their apparent certainty these constitution-makers knew they were engaged in a great experiment. "To object against the present constitution because it is a *novelty*, is to give one of the best indirect reasons for trying it," Paine said in 1778.

Embedded somewhere among these early constitutions, but not in any single one, were a variety of political experiments. Pennsylvania introduced the constitutional convention, Massachusetts the ratifying convention, New York the popular election of the governor, Delaware the provision for amendment.

Politically, then, it would seem to me that the American Revolution inaugurated several revolutionary concepts and practices. But the Revolution was to be broader than politics. To attack the monarch was to attack the basic institution around which life was organized in the 18th century. Once a man accepted the principle of a republican form of government he had committed himself to more than a political revolution. He must revolutionize society, too. His entire way of looking at the world around him had now changed.

Liberty, as Bernard Bailyn has remarked, was contagious, and men everywhere in America began to question all sides of American life. Jefferson, as I have remarked, called for reform in voting qualifications. Ezra Stiles, a minister in Newport, R.I., had previously felt no uneasiness about the slaves he owned until it struck him that if it were wrong for Britain to enslave America, it must be equally wrong for Americans to enslave Africans. The thought impelled him, like Rush, to free his Negroes.

This zeal to reform all America was bound to be frustrated, but to admit its failure to be realized is not to deny it existed. How many revolutions achieve all their goals?

Those who favor calling the Revolution a war for independence have made the point that the ideal of equality, which once seemed a product of the war, was indeed a fixture of American life long before the war. This is true. A visiting French aristocrat found this out long before the Revolution ended. "When you travel about this land," he observed, "it very commonly happens that after you have been some time in bed, a stranger of any condition (for there is little distinction here) comes into the room, pulls off his clothes, and places himself, without ceremony, between your sheets."

This same Frenchman found only one thing gave distinction in American society—money. When he wondered why Mrs. Robert Morris was given precedence at every dinner she attended, he checked and learned it was because "she is the richest woman in the city, and all ranks here being equal, men follow their natural bent by giving preference to wealth." When Mrs. Morris' husband became bankrupt, her social standing vanished with his money.

Equality may have been a fact of American life before the war, but it became after the war a social principle to be guarded with the passion of America's political principles. A congressional plan to give revolutionary officers five years' extra pay failed to pass because some saw it favored one class against another. The Society of the Cincinnati, whose members were limited to army officers and who were allowed to pass their membership on to their descendants, was censured as an attempt to establish a hereditary aristocracy.

The effect of the Revolution on the plain people is hard to judge, for they left few records behind. The effect on the colonial elite, the bright able men whose careers had been blocked, is easier to judge. They were elated.

Here among the rising elite was where the Revolution worked a real social revolution. "Among us no one can exercise any authority by virtue of birth," said one young man, thinking of what life had been like under the royal governments. "All start equal in the race of life."

The Unprofessional Soldier

DANIEL J. BOORSTIN

• Anti-war demonstrations, draft-card burnings, desertions to
Sweden, and flights to Canada are constant reminders that
United States participation in a deadly and expensive war
far from American shores is not popular with many citizens.
Although such actions are often considered as a "sign of the
times," Americans have rarely been overly eager to march off
to war or to accept the discipline of military life.

During the War of 1812 bounties of money, land, and
clothing were promised to recruits to stimulate voluntary
enlistments, but the army was consistently short of men.
Although the free population of the United States outnumbered that of Canada by twelve to one, two months after the
initiation of hostilities Henry Adams reported that Canadian
forces outnumbered the Americans "at every point of danger
on the frontier."

Before the advent of national conscription on March 3,
1863, the reluctance of American men to arise to the call of
the Union was frequently evident. On July 2, 1862, President
Abraham Lincoln appealed to the states to raise "three hundred thousand more," yet state-wide drafts and other induce-
ments produced only 88,000. Soon after the draft laws went
into effect, Irish mobs in New York City gave expression to
their resentment by burning buildings and attacking free
blacks. The rioters objected to the fact that well-to-do citizens could and did avoid military duty either by paying fees
or hiring substitutes. During the first four months of the
application of the law, ninety-eight registrars were killed by
indignant citizens. The Confederacy also permitted the hiring of substitutes for a time and exempted the owners of
twenty or more slaves from military duty.

The Spanish-American War and World Wars I and II were probably the most widely supported American wars. In World War I, for example, desertions were less common than in any previous American military action. But even then, when conscientious objection was not recognized by draft law, men used marriage and other less severe measures to escape the draft.

Once in combat, Americans have been as courageous and effective as the soldiers of any other nation. In World War II German prisoners testified "to the fear of these silent soldiers moving remorselessly forward that grew in the ranks of the German divisions." Yet Americans anxiously returned to their civilian roles as soon as hostilities ended. The tradition of the citizen-soldier, of the man who goes to war unwillingly but with the firm expectation of victory, is a long one in American history. Daniel J. Boorstin explains the role of the militia in the Revolutionary War and suggests that military leaders have often been popular in American society precisely because they were expected to be "Unprofessional soldiers."

The belief that American wars would always be fought by "embattled farmers" was rooted in the earliest facts of American life. Military men were to be simply citizens in arms. The military caste, the Man-on-Horseback, the Palace Revolution, the Coup d'État, the tug of war between army and civil government—these recurring motifs in continental European political life did not appear on the American scene. Civilian control over the army, clearly asserted in the Federal Constitution, merely declared what was already one of the firmest institutions of colonial life.

The typical American view of the military appeared in Doddridge's description of the backwoodsmen who "formed the cordon along the Ohio river, on the frontiers of Pennsylvania, Virginia and Kentucky, which defended the country against the attacks of the Indians during the revolutionary war. They were the janizaries of the country, that is, they were soldiers when they chose to be so, and when they chose laid down their arms. Their military service was voluntary, and of course received no pay."

Long before the end of the colonial period, British politicians and professional soldiers had learned that they could not rely on Americans to fill the ranks of the regular army stationed in America. While the backwoodsman with his sharpshooting rifle was ready and able to defend his home, he was intractable within a European-type professional army. The armed civilians of the separate colonies, which in their intense localism refused to cooperate in any large strategy, were inadequate to the large tasks of colonial defense. If the British government hoped to protect the colonies by preventing the accumulation of offensive French military strength, they had to send in a professional army from the outside. The capture of Louisbourg by New Englanders in 1745 was the only instance in the colonial period of a successful large-scale military operation by provincial fighters—and even that was the product not of wise planning but of lucky coincidence.

When General Braddock made his preparations for the disastrous campaign of 1755, he put relatively small reliance on American troops. Even at that he was expecting too much. The nucleus of his army was soldiers of regular regiments of the British Army, supposed to be brought up to full strength by American recruits, to be supported by voluntary financial aid from the colonial assemblies, and to be partly provisioned by the colonies. But Braddock was disappointed: few recruits were raised, the assemblies refused substantial assistance, and wagons and supplies were offered only at exorbitant rates. Characteristically, the northern colonies voted instead to set up a wholly provincial army under a general of their own choosing. This foreshadowed the difficulties which Lord Loudoun would meet on a larger scale a few years later and which would dramatize the divergence of American from European ways of war.

Loudoun's activities comprised the greatest British effort before the Revolution to control and centralize American military activities. According to plans made in advance, he arrived in America in 1756 carrying a broad commission to organize a force against the French and Indians; he was supposed to command a regular army of nearly fourteen thousand men (two-thirds of the privates besides replacements to be colonials). During two years of recruitment, the British, using dubious methods, managed to enlist about 7500 Americans; during the same period the British Isles supplied only about 4500. The year 1757 showed a decided reversal of proportions: in that year only about 1200 men were recruited in the colonies, while 11,000 came from England. Loudoun, with the hoped-for acquiescence of the separate colonial governments, was supposed to be supreme commander of all local forces, including, of course, their militia. But the more Loudoun learned of colonial troops and colonial ways, the less he came to rely on them—whether as recruits for the ranks of his regular regiments or as supporting forces organized in their own militia. "The King must trust in this country to himself and those he sends," Lord Loudoun wrote back from America as early as September 1756, ". . . for this Country will not run when he calls."

Everything that Loudoun, with the experienced eye of a professional soldier, saw of the American provincial militias appalled him. Upon his arrival, there were about seven thousand militiamen occupying the colonies' northern forts. These men had been raised, and their officers commissioned, each by his separate province; for all practical purposes each group was responsible only to its own distinct government. When Loudoun and his subordinates inspected the camp commanded by General John Winslow (who had been commissioned by the Governors of Massachusetts, Connecticut, and New York), they were horrified by the absence of decent military order or even rudimentary sanitation. They saw a hundred graves dug in a day for men dead of disease. "The fort stinks enough to cause an infection," Loudoun heard from Fort William Henry, "they have all their sick in it. The camp nastier than anything I could conceive, their necessary houses, kitchens, graves and places for slaughtering cattle, all mixed through their encampment." Deserters were only mildly punished. Loudoun was shocked to see men firing their guns at random after drill, sleeping on post, and taking pot shots at game while they were on the march. But the elected officers would seldom risk unpopularity by punishing offenders.

No commander in his right mind would admit men with such a conception of an army into a regiment of well-disciplined regulars. And why, indeed, should any American put himself under the strict discipline of the British Army? Everything was better in the provincial militias: a Massachusetts private soldier received all of 10¼d sterling a day while a British regular private received no more than 4d; in addition, the provincial soldier received an annual bounty for reënlistment. Supplies for the provincials looked like luxuries to the regulars. The militiaman not only received a greater staple allowance, but after one summer's service, he was allowed to keep his hatchet, blanket, and knapsack—and he soon established the profitable custom of taking his musket home with him. He could count on his sugar, ginger, rum, and molasses; and his marching allowance was three times that of a British regular.

This life of a provincial militiaman was free-and-easy compared to that of the regular, who might be punished with flogging, or be forced to enlist for life in the West Indies. It was so free-and-easy in fact that the commander of provincial troops never really knew how many men he had at his disposal. The militiaman preferred to stay close to home, so that he could return to his family in case of need. When the General Court of Massachusetts voted troops for the expedition to Crown Point in northeastern New York, they expressly provided that the men "shall not be compelled to march southward of Albany, or westward of Schenechtedy." "The Troops are constantly coming & going," an observer wrote of General Johnson's New York army, "ill arm'd, ill cloath'd & worse disciplined, some having served their time out, as they phrase it, and some commencing fresh men. Never to be sure was such a motly Herd, almost every man his own master & a General."

The "leveling spirit" of the Americans was notorious among British officers. "Our Militia is under no kind of discipline. . . ." complained Cadwallader Colden to Lord Halifax in 1754. "The Inhabitants of the Northern Colonies are all so nearly on a level, and a licentiousness, under the notion of liberty, so generally prevails, that they are impatient under all kind of superiority and authority." "The Officers of the Army with very few Exceptions," a colonial observer noted of such provincial troops, "are utter Strangers to Military Life and most of them in no Respect superior to the Men they are put over, They are like the heads and indeed are the heads of a Mob." Such "officers" had long been snubbed by British regulars. In 1741 in the expedition against Cartagena in the Caribbean, officers from Virginia, including even the experienced and highly competent Governor Gooch, had been passed over for promotion and brazenly mistreated. George Washington himself had traveled alone half-way across the colonies to settle just such a question concerning his own military rank. The established policy repeated by the Duke of Cumberland in 1754 ordered "that all Troops serving by Commissions signed by Us, or by Our General Commanding in Chief in North America, shall take Rank before all Troops which may serve by Commission from any of the Governors or Councils of Our Provinces in North America: And It is Our further Pleasure, that the Generals and Field Officers of the Provincial Troops shall have no Rank with the Generals & Field Officers who serve by Commissions from Us." Loudoun brought with him to America a modified order allowing colonial officers more rank, but by then it was too late.

There was not a single problem that plagued Loudoun in the French and Indian War that did not also trouble Washington in the War of Independence. Washington, trying to raise a unified Continental Army from unmilitary Americans, now stood in the shoes of Lord Loudoun. Although the "cause" was different, the difficulties were the same. The Continental Army, like the British Regular Army twenty years earlier, had to compete for men against the separate state militias, and Washington had only slightly more success. Had the American cause been forced to depend on an American regular army, the outcome would have been even more doubtful and drawn-out. Washington, however, took wise advantage of his opportunity to fight the war seriatim—first in New England, then in the Middle Colonies, then in the South—rather than all-at-once, as the French and Indian Wars had been fought. This made the dispersed militia more useful and his smaller army more effective.

The unseemly disputes over rank and precedence, in which regular British officers had lorded it over mere militiamen, were reënacted with the officers of the Continental line now assuming the old airs of the regulars. The Congress and the States showed democratic prodigality; they lavished military titles on mere able-bodied citizens, regardless of competence. "My blacksmith is a captain," De Kalb reported in amazement. To avoid offense, it was always safer to assume that anybody was entitled to be addressed as a high officer. "Not an hour passes," Washington wrote to the President of the Continental Congress (Aug. 3, 1778), "without new applications and new complaints about rank. . . . We can scarcely form a Court Martial or parade a detachment in any instance, without a warm discussion on the subject of precedence." When Colonel Crafts of the militia and Colonel Jackson of the Continental army arrived to act as pall-bearers at the funeral of a fellow-officer, Crafts as the older man claimed the right to walk first, but Jackson argued that as a Continental officer he was entitled to precedence. Neither gave in, and Crafts and his friends walked out on the funeral.

Even Washington's patience wore thin; but since local prides were not to be overcome, he learned to live with them and somehow to harness them in the common cause. "I have labored, ever since I have been in the service," Washington wrote at the end of 1776, "to discourage all kinds of local attachments and distinctions of country [i.e. of State], denominating the whole by the greater name of *American*, but I have found it impossible to overcome prejudices; and, under the new establishment, I conceive it best to stir up an emulation; in order to do which would it not be better for each State to furnish, though not to appoint, their own brigadiers?" In 1780, to the inquiries of the Congress about his problems of promotion and rank, he replied: "If in all cases ours was *one* army, or *thirteen* armies allied for the common defence, there would be no difficulty in solving your question; but we are occasionally both, and I should not be much out if I were to say, that we are sometimes *neither*, but a compound of *both*."

All the American armies were competing against each other for men, for officers, for rank, and for glory. Privates from New England were being offered higher pay than those from the Middle States. Massachusetts even offered to pay its men by lunar rather than calendar months in order to secure a competitive advantage. This particular trick Washington stigmatized as the "most fatal stab to the peace of this Army, that ever was given. . . . Lord North himself could not have devised a more effectual blow to the recruiting Service." Problems were compounded by the familiar "leveling" tendencies of the Americans; by their refusal to allow a sufficiently higher pay to officers, they stirred discontent and bred an unmilitary familiarity between officers and men.

The widespread fear of a permanent professional army increased the difficulties. John Adams declared it safer in the long run to put public faith in a temporary though less effective militia. "Although it may cost us more, and we may put now and then a battle to hazard by the method we are in, yet we shall be less in danger of corruption and violence from a standing army, and our militia will acquire courage, experience, discipline, and hardiness in actual service. I wish every man upon the continent was a soldier, and obliged, upon occasion, to fight and determined to conquer or to die. Flight was unknown to the Romans. I wish it was to Americans." Proposals to offer long-term pensions to officers, in order to attract better men and to raise their morale, were widely opposed. Elbridge Gerry listed the reasons (Jan. 13, 1778): "the infant state of the country, its aversion to placemen and pensioners, whereby Great Britain is likely to lose her liberty, the equality of the officers and soldiers of some States, before the war."

Short-term enlistments (sometimes for as little as three months) expressed both the widespread fear of a professional standing army and the assumption that an army would be superfluous the day after the war was won. Washington repeatedly complained that this was the core of his problem. For example, in a circular (Oct. 18, 1780) to the several States from his headquarters near Passaic, he said:

> I am religiously persuaded that the duration of the war, and the greatest part of the Misfortunes, and perplexities we have hitherto experienced, are chiefly to be attributed to temporary inlistments. . . . A moderate, compact force, on a permanent establishment capable of acquiring the discipline essential to military operations, would have been able to make head against the Enemy, without comparison better than the throngs of Militia, which have been at certain periods not in the feild, but on their way to, and from the feild: for from that want of perseverance which characterises all Militia, and of that coercion which cannot be exercised upon them it has always been found impracticable to detain the greatest part of them in service even for the term, for which they have been called out; and this has been commonly so short, that we have had a great proportion of the time, two sets of men to feed and pay, one coming to the Army, and the other going from it.

Men went home just as they were beginning to understand their duties, and it was often necessary to recruit a new army in the face of the enemy. More than one American military defeat can be explained by the transient character of the army. General Richard Montgomery rushed into his disastrous assault on Quebec in late December 1775 because the enlistments of all his New England troops would expire at midnight on December 31, and he was sure they would not stay with him a day longer.

The unreliability and lack of discipline of the American armed citizenry, which had been so hastily gathered into military ranks, haunted brave Revolutionary commanders from Washington down to lieutenants in the field, and made large-scale planning mere wishful thinking. Time after time militia fled the battlefield, spreading defeatism as they went. "America," warned Washington, "has been almost amused out of her Liberties" by the proponents of the militia. "I solemnly declare I never was witness to a single instance, that can countenance an opinion of Militia or raw Troops being fit for the real business of fighting. I have found them useful as light Parties to skirmish in the woods, but incapable of making or sustaining a serious attack. . . . The late battle of Camden is a melancholly comment upon this doctrine. The Militia fled at the first fire, and left the Continental Troops surrounded on every side, and overpowered by numbers to combat for safety instead of victory." "Great god," exclaimed Daniel Morgan on Feb. 1, 1781, only a few days after his victory over Tarleton, "what is the reason we cant Have more men in the field— so many men in the country Nearby idle for want of employment." At this critical moment in the War, when Greene was retreating before Cornwallis, Edward Stevens vainly appealed to his troops.

> After crossing the Yadkin we could not have Paraded a greater Force than Eight Hundred for Action if even that Including Militia and all and a great part of the number was the Militia under me whose times were out. I saw the greatest necessity of these men remaining a few days till the Troops from General Greens Camp could get up, and this the General requested of me to endeavour to bring about. I had them paraded and addressed them on the Subject. But to my great mortification and astonishment scarce a man would agree to it, And gave for answer he was a good Soldier that Served his time out. If the Salvation of the Country had depended on their staying Ten or Fifteen days, I dont believe they would have done it. Militia wont do. Their greatest Study is to Rub through their Tower [Tour] of Duty with whole Bones.

But many militiamen were not this scrupulous of their duty; they often went home before their term was up. Desertions were commonplace. It is hard to assess the military tactics of some battles because one can never be sure how many of the "losses" of the Revolutionary army were due to desertion rather than to death or capture. Within a few weeks before the Battle of Bennington on August 16, 1777, more than four hundred men deserted—or, more accurately, disappeared. At the siege of Newport, about the same time, five thousand militiamen deserted within a few days, so weakening Sullivan's forces that he had to abandon any idea of attack. On many occasions—for example, near Savannah in March 1779, at Johnstown in October 1781, and at other places too numerous to mention—large numbers of militia fled in panic. Although the Americans had outnumbered the British by more than fifty per cent at Guilford Court House on March 15, 1781, the wholesale flight of the militia to the woods gave victory to the British. The experienced General Daniel Morgan had shrewdly foreseen just this when he warned General Nathanael Greene against the "great number of militia" and advised, "If they fight, you beat Cornwallis, if not, he will beat you." "Put the . . . militia in the centre, with some picked troops in their rear with orders to shoot down the first man that runs." Greene followed Morgan's advice, but the anxiety of the North Carolina and Virginia militia prevailed.

How could such an ill-assorted, ill-disciplined, and ill-supplied army succeed against the well-organized forces of one of the great military powers? How, indeed, can we account for the final victory? Many acts of heroism, courage, and sacrifice embellished the records of the fighting Americans. The unorthodox imagination of amateur American generals, in sharp contrast to the professional rigidity of the British command, gave the colonials an unexpected advantage. But it is still hard to explain why the British surrendered so quickly after Yorktown. Today the most persuasive answer is not that the Americans won but that the British lost—or perhaps that they simply gave up, having seen the long-run hopelessness of their cause. The American terrain (together with the colonial dispersion, which meant that there was no jugular vein to be cut by British force) led the British to realize that to subdue America was beyond their means. Within the first four years of the Revolution, every one of the most populous towns—Boston, New York, Philadelphia, and Charleston—had fallen to the British and had been occupied by their regular troops, but always without decisive effect. The American center was everywhere and nowhere—in each man himself. In addition, the French brought crucial aid to the American militia and irregulars, and the spectre of a permanent American alliance with France haunted the British Empire.

Perhaps the most typical and most ominous of the military events of the war was the abrupt disbanding of the army. In January, 1781—ten months before Cornwallis' surrender at Yorktown—mutiny shook the army in Pennsylvania; again, on the brink of peace in June 1783, mutinous soldiers, in control of the powder magazines and public officers at the seat of the Continental Congress in Philadelphia, threatened to use force to get their wages. It was in the shadow of such disorder that the Continental Army was hastily dispersed and that General Washington on December fourth bade a tearful farewell to his officers. Nothing was more American about the Revolution than this conclusion of it, when armed citizens impatiently dissolved themselves back into the populace. In this, as in later wars in American history, "the end of the war" and the end of the army were substantially, and disastrously, synonymous.

In American folklore it is fitting that the first call to arms, the rousing of "embattled farmers," the sudden appearance of Minute Men, together with Washington's Farewell and the last dispersion of the army, should remain the most permanent and the most moving symbols. The story of the actual administration of the Army is dismal and discreditable—almost unprecedented in the annals of war.

Yet the very weaknesses of the professional army had already foreshadowed strengths in American institutions. Unmilitary Americans freely chose a general for their first President. Washington might become "first in war, first in peace, and first in the hearts of his countrymen," but the political power given to a military leader meant something very different here from what it might have meant elsewhere. The American military ideal was not Caesar but Cincinnatus, not the skilled general glorying in the tasks of warfare to which he gave his life, but the planter who had unwillingly left his tobacco fields.

When, near the end of the war, American officers tried to set up an organization to perpetuate their comradeship, their memories, and their tradition (and perhaps their political influence), they significantly chose to call themselves the Society of the Cincinnati. Washington assumed its leadership—though only with the greatest reluctance, for he was suspicious of the organization and hoped to see it soon dissolved. Among the people at large it aroused violent fears of a military caste; they saw in such a hereditary military society a dangerous center of aristocracy, a focus of monarchic conspiracy. The Society was so congenial to the monarchic spirit that King Louis XVI of France authorized his officers to form a branch chapter and to wear the Order of the Cincinnati as a military decoration.

Long after the Society of the Cincinnati had faded from the public memory, another American military institution reached into many American homes. This was the Purple Heart Badge of Military Merit, which Washington established by a general order of Aug. 7, 1782:

> The General ever desirous to cherish a virtuous ambition in his soldiers, as well as to foster and encourage every species of Military merit, directs that whenever any singularly meritorious action is performed, the author of it shall be permitted to wear on his facings over the left breast, the figure of a heart in purple cloth or silk, edged with narrow lace or binding. Not only instances of unusual gallantry, but also of extraordinary fidelity and essential Service in any way shall meet with a due reward. . . . Men who have merited this last distinction to be suffered to pass all guards and sentinels which officers are permitted to do.

> The road to glory in a patriot army and a free country is thus open to all—this order is also to have retrospect to the earliest stages of the war, and to be considered as a permanent one.

Even though the Federal Constitution later gave the power to wage war to the central government, the American army was never fully unified. State militias, under their later guise of the "national guard," remained important; they helped keep alive a spirit of local allegiance and a variety of practice and military standards which eventually created all kinds of problems. The peacetime regional nucleus of the militia or "national guard" stayed together through a Civil War and two World Wars, so that many men continued to fight beside their neighbors.

Starting with Washington himself, American history would offer again and again—especially after the decline of the Virginia Dynasty —examples of men whose fame on the battlefield eventually led them to the highest civil office. Even in Great Britain, where there was little fear of military coups d'état during the 18th and 19th centuries, military men rarely became prime ministers; turning military success into a political career was almost unheard of there. But in America this became common: the prominent examples—Jackson, William Henry Harrison, Taylor, Grant, Theodore Roosevelt, and Eisenhower—come quickly to mind. Some of these men had begun, not in the ranks of the regular army, but in the local militia. And their military exploits —far from seeming mere success in a specialized profession— actually attested their success as undifferentiated Americans. Precisely because there was no military caste, the citizen-soldier easily found a place in American political life.

Watermelon Armies and Whiskey Boys

GERALD CARSON

• Although Americans hold ambivalent views about alco-
holic beverages, it cannot be denied that whiskey has played
an important role in our culture from its very inception. The
Pilgrims carried liquor with them on the Mayflower, and
Congress itself voted to provide supplies of spirits to the
American army during Revolutionary times. During the
1700's whiskey was said to be vital to the workers in the
southern states because of the hot climate.

To the Scotch-Irish of Pennsylvania, whiskey was not only
an economic commodity but as necessary to their lives as
Bibles and plows. Thus, when Alexander Hamilton proposed
an internal revenue tax on distilled liquors, rumblings of dis-
satisfaction arose from the western Pennsylvania frontier.
Because they based their livelihood on distilling grain rather
than transporting the crop across the mountains, the farmers regarded the tax as discriminatory and leveled their shot-
guns at the revenue agents who came to collect. Public pro-
tests erupted, thousands marched on Pittsburgh, and there
were talks of secession from the United States. Ultimately,
President George Washington sent in federal troops.

Alexander Hamilton thought that the use of the army
would illustrate the power of the newly created government
to enforce the law. As you read Carson's witty and colorful
account of the Whiskey Rebellion of 1794, consider the question of the use of federal troops to force compliance with a
locally unpopular national policy. Does the use of military
force, as Hamilton suggested, increase the citizen's respect for
and adherence to the national laws? What similarities, if any,
do you find between the quelling of the Whiskey Rebellion
of 1794 and the use of the military to enforce integrated edu-

cation in Little Rock, Arkansas, in 1957 and to dispel youthful protesters at the Democratic National Convention in
Chicago in August 1968?

When one recalls that the President of the United States, the Secretary of War, the Secretary of the Treasury and the governors of four
states once mobilized against the farmers of western Pennsylvania
almost as large an army as ever took the field in the Revolutionary
War, the event appears at first glance as one of the more improbable
episodes in the annals of this country. Thirteen thousand grenadiers,
dragoons, foot soldiers and pioneers, a train of artillery with six-
pounders, mortars and several "grasshoppers," equipped with mountains of ammunition, forage, baggage and a bountiful stock of tax-
paid whiskey, paraded over the mountains to Pittsburgh against a
gaggle of homespun rebels who had already dispersed.

Yet the march had a rationale. President George Washington and
his Secretary of the Treasury, Alexander Hamilton, moved to counter
civil commotion with overwhelming force because they well understood that the viability of the United States Constitution was involved.
Soon after he assumed his post at the Treasury, Hamilton had proposed, to the astonishment of the country, that the United States
should meet fully and promptly its financial obligations, including the
assumption of the debts contracted by the states in the struggle for
independence. The money was partly to be raised by laying an excise
tax upon distilled spirits. The tax, which was universally detested in
the West—"odious" was the word most commonly used to describe
it—became law on March 3, 1791.

The news of the passage of the measure was greeted with a roar
of indignation in the back country settlements. The duty was laid
uniformly upon all the states, as the Constitution provided. If the
West had to pay more, Secretary Hamilton explained, it was only
because it used more whiskey. The East could, if it so desired,
forgo beverage spirits and fall back on cider and beer. The South
could not. It had neither orchards nor breweries. To Virginia and
Maryland the excise tax appeared to be as unjust and oppressive as

the well-remembered Molasses Act and the tea duties of George III. "The time will come," predicted fiery James Jackson of Georgia in the House of Representatives, "when a shirt shall not be washed without an excise."

Kentucky, then thinly settled, but already producing its characteristic hand-made, whole-souled liquor from planished copper stills, was of the opinion that the law was unconstitutional. Deputy revenue collectors throughout the Bluegrass region were assaulted, their papers stolen, their horses' ears cropped and their saddles cut to pieces. On one wild night the people of Lexington dragged a stuffed dummy through the streets and hanged in effigy Colonel Thomas Marshall, the chief collector for the district.

Yet in no other place did popular fury rise so high, spread so rapidly, involve a whole population so completely, express so many assorted grievances, as in the Pennsylvania frontier counties of Fayette, Allegheny, Westmoreland and Washington. In these counties, around 1791, a light plume of wood smoke rose from the chimneys of no less than five thousand log stillhouses. The rates went into effect on July first. The whiskey maker could choose whether he would pay a yearly levy on his still capacity or a gallonage tax ranging from nine to eleven cents on his actual production.

Before the month was out, "committees of correspondence," in the old Revolutionary phrase, were speeding horsemen over the ridges and through the valleys to arouse the people to arm and assemble. The majority, but not all, of the men who made the whiskey decided to "forbear" from paying the tax. The revenue officers were thoroughly worked over. Robert Johnson, for example, collector for Washington and Allegheny counties, was waylaid near Pigeon Creek by a mob disguised in women's clothing. They cut off his hair, gave him a coat of tar and feathers and stole his horse.

The Pennsylvania troubles were rooted in the economic importance and impregnable social position of mellow old Monongahela rye whiskey. In 1825, for instance, when the Philadelphia Society for Promoting Agriculture offered a gold medal to the person in Pennsylvania who carried on large-scale farming operations without providing ardent spirits for his farm workers, the medal could not be awarded. There were no entries for the uncoveted honor.

The frontier people had been reared from childhood on the

family jug of farmer whiskey. They found the taste pleasant, the effect agreeable. Whiskey was usually involved when there was kissing or fighting. It beatified the rituals of birth and death. The doctor kept a bottle in his office for his own use under the deceptive label "Arsenic —Deadly poison." The lawyer produced the bottle when the papers were signed. Whiskey was available in the prothonotary's office when the trial-list was made up. Jurors got their dram, and the constable drew his ration for his services on election day. The hospitable barrel and the tin cup were the mark of the successful political candidate. The United States Army issued a gill to a man every day. Ministers of the gospel were paid in rye whiskey, for they were shepherds of a devout flock, Scotch Presbyterians mostly, who took their Bible straight, especially where it said: "Give strong drink unto him that is ready to perish, and wine unto those that be of heavy hearts."

With grain the most abundant commodity west of the mountains, the farmers could eat it or drink it, but they couldn't sell it in distant markets unless it was reduced in bulk and enhanced in value. A Pennsylvania farmer's "best holt," then, was whiskey. A pack-horse could move only four bushels of grain. But it could carry twenty-four bushels if it was condensed into two kegs of whiskey slung across its back, while the price of the goods would double when they reached the eastern markets. So whiskey became the remittance of the fringe settlements for salt, sugar, nails, bar iron, pewter plates, powder and shot. Along the western rivers where men saw few shilling pieces, a gallon of good, sound rye whiskey was a stable measure of value.

The bitter resistance of the western men to the whiskey tax involved both practical considerations and principles. First, the excise payment was due and must be paid in hard money as soon as the water-white distillate flowed from the condensing coil. The principle concerned the whole repulsive idea of an internal revenue levy. The settlers of western Pennsylvania were a bold, hardy, emigrant race who brought with them bitter memories of oppression under the excise laws in Scotland and Ireland, involving invasion of their homes, confiscation of their property and a system of paid informers. Revenue collectors were social outcasts in a society which warmly seconded Doctor Samuel Johnson's definition of excise: "a hateful tax levied upon commodities, and adjudged not by the common judges of property, but wretches hired by those to whom excise is paid."

The whiskey boys of Pennsylvania saw it as simply a matter of sound Whig doctrine to resist the exciseman as he made his rounds with Dicas' hydrometer to measure the proof of the whiskey and his marking iron to brand the casks with his findings. Earlier, Pennsylvania had taxed spirits. But whiskey produced for purely private use was exempt. William Findley of Westmoreland County, a member of Congress at the time and a sympathetic interpreter of the western point of view, looked into this angle. To his astonishment, he learned that all of the whiskey distilled in the west was for purely personal use. So far as the state's excise tax was concerned, or any other tax, for that matter, the sturdy Celtic peoples of the Monongahela region had cheerfully returned to nature: they just didn't pay. About every sixth man made whiskey. But all were involved in the problem, since the other five took their grain to the stillhouse where the master distiller turned it into liquid form.

The state had been lenient. But now matters had taken a more serious turn. The new federal government in Philadelphia was dividing the whole country up into "districts" for the purpose of collecting the money. And the districts were subdivided into smaller "surveys." The transmontane Pennsylvanians found themselves in the grip of something known as the fourth survey, with General John Neville, hitherto a popular citizen and leader, getting ready to enforce the law, with a reward paid to informers and a percentage to the collectors, who appeared to be a rapacious set.

The first meeting of public protest against the 1791 federal tax was held at Redstone Old Fort, now Brownsville. The proceedings were moderate on that occasion, and scarcely went beyond the right of petition. Another meeting in August, more characteristic of others which were to follow, was radical in tone, disorderly, threatening. It passed resolves to the effect that any person taking office under the revenue law was an enemy of society.

When warrants were issued in the affair of Robert Johnson, the process server was robbed, beaten, tarred and feathered and left tied to a tree in the forest. As the inspectors' offices were established, they were systematically raided. Liberty poles reappeared as whiskey poles. The stills of operators who paid the tax were riddled with bullets in attacks sardonically known as "mending" the still. This led to a popular description of the Whiskey Boys as "Tom the Tinker's Men," an ironical reference to the familiar, itinerant repairer of pots and kettles. Notices proposing measures for thwarting the law, or aimed at coercing the distillers, were posted on trees or published in the *Pittsburgh Gazette* over the signature, "Tom the Tinker," nom de plume of the insurgent John Holcroft and other anti-tax agitators. Findley, who tried to build a bridge of understanding between the backwoodsmen and the central government, described the outbreak as not the result of any concerted plan, but rather as a flame, "an infatuation almost incredible."

An additional grievance grew out of the circumstance that offenders were required to appear in the federal court at Philadelphia, three hundred miles away. The whiskey-makers saw this distant government as being no less oppressive than one seated in London, and often drew the parallel. The Scotch-Irish of western Pennsylvania were, in sum, anti-federalist, anti-tax, and it may be added, anti-Indian. West of Pittsburgh lay Indian country. The men of the west held to a simple concept of how to solve the Indian problem: extermination. The Indians had the same program, in reverse, and were getting better results. The bungling campaigns, which generals Hamar and St. Clair had conducted in the early 1790's made the people of the fringe settlements despair of the ability of the Union to protect them.

Congress amended the excise tax law in 1792 and again in 1794 to lighten the burden on country distillers. A further conciliatory step was taken. To ease the hardships of the judicial process, Congress gave to the state courts jurisdiction in excise offenses so that accused persons might be tried in their own vicinity. But some fifty or sixty writs already issued and returnable at Philadelphia resulted in men being carried away from their fields during harvest time. This convinced the insurgents that the federalist East was seeking a pretext to discipline the democratic West.

One day in July, while the papers were being served, William Miller, a delinquent farmer-distiller, and political supporter of General Neville, saw the General riding up his lane accompanied by a stranger who turned out to be a United States marshal from Philadelphia. The marshal unlimbered an official paper and began to read a summons. It ordered said Miller peremptorily to "set aside all manner of business and excuses" and appear in his "proper person" before a Philadelphia judge. Miller had been planning to sell his property and remove to Kentucky. The cost of the trip to Philadelphia and the fine for which he was liable would eat up the value of his land and betterments. The farm was as good as gone.

"I felt my blood boil at seeing General Neville along to pilot the sheriff to my very door," Miller said afterward. "I felt myself mad with passion."

As Neville and the marshal rode away, a party from the county militia which was mustered at Mingo Creek fired upon them, but there were no casualties. When the General reached Bower Hill, his country home above the Chartiers Valley, another party under the command of John Holcroft awaited him there and demanded his commission and official papers. The demand was refused and both sides began to shoot. As the rebels closed in on the main house, a flanking fire came from the Negro cabins on the plantation. The Whiskey Boys were driven off with one killed and four wounded.

The next day, Major James McFarlane, a veteran of the Revolution, led an attack in force upon Neville's painted and wall-papered mansion, furnished with such marvels as carpets, mirrors, pictures and prints and an eight-day clock. The house was now defended by a dozen soldiers from Fort Fayette at Pittsburgh. A fire-fight followed during which a soldier was shot and McFarlane was killed—by treachery, the rebels said, when a white flag was displayed. The soldiers surrendered and were either released or allowed to escape. Neville was not found, but his cabins, barns, outbuildings and finally the residence were all burned to the ground. Stocks of grain were destroyed, all fences leveled, as the victors broke up the furniture, liberated the mirrors and clock, and distributed Neville's supply of liquor to the mob.

The funeral of McFarlane caused great excitement. Among those present were Hugh Henry Brackenridge, author, lawyer and one of the western moderates, and David Bradford, prosecuting attorney for Washington County. The former wished to find ways to reduce the tension; the latter to increase it. Bradford was a rash, impetuous Marylander, ambitious for power and position. Some thought him a second-rate lawyer. Others disagreed. They said he was third-rate. But he had a gift for rough mob eloquence. Bradford had already robbed the United States mails to find out what information was being sent east against the conspirators. He had already called for the people to make a choice of "submission or opposition . . . with *head, heart, hand* and *voice*."

At Major McFarlane's funeral service Bradford worked powerfully upon the feelings of his sympathizers as he described "the murder of McFarlane." Brackenridge also spoke, using wit and drollery to let down the pressure and to make palatable his warning to the insurgents that they were flirting with the possibility of being hanged. But the temper of the throng was for Bradford, clearly revealed in the epitaph which was set over McFarlane's grave. It said "He fell . . . by the hands of an unprincipled villain in the support of what he supposed to be the rights of his country."

The high-water mark of the insurrection was the occupation of Pittsburgh. After the fight and the funeral, Bradford called out the militia regiments of the four disaffected counties. They were commanded to rendezvous at Braddock's Feld, near Pittsburgh, with arms, full equipment and four days' rations. At the field there was a great beating of drums, much marching and counter-marching, almost a holiday spirit. Men in hunting shirts practiced shooting at the mark until a dense pall of smoke hung over the plain, as there had been thirty-nine years before at the time of General Braddock's disaster. There were between five and seven thousand men on the field, many meditating in an ugly mood upon their enemies holed up in the town, talking of storming Fort Fayette and burning Pittsburgh as "a second Sodom."

Bradford's dream was the establishment of an independent state with himself cast as a sort of Washington of the West. Elected by acclaim as Major General, he dashed about the field on a superb horse in a fancy uniform, his sword flashing, plumes floating out from his hat. As he harangued the multitude, Bradford received applications for commissions in the service of—what? No one quite knew.

Marching in good order, strung out over two and a half miles of road, the rebels advanced on August first toward Pittsburgh in what was hopefully interpreted as a "visit," though the temper of the whiskey soldiers was perhaps nearer to that of one man who twirled his hat on the muzzle of his rifle and shouted, "I have a bad hat now, but I expect to have a better one soon." While the panic-stricken burghers buried the silver and locked up the girls, the mob marched

in on what is now Fourth Avenue to the vicinity of the present Baltimore and Ohio Railroad station. A reception committee extended
nervous hospitality in the form of hams, poultry, dried venison, bear
meat, water and whiskey. They agreed to banish certain citizens obnoxious to the insurrectionists. One building on a suburban farm was
burned. Another attempt at arson failed to come off. The day cost
Brackenridge four barrels of prime Monongahela. It was better, he
reflected, "to be employed in extinguishing the fire of their thirst
than of my house." Pittsburgh was fortunate in getting the main body
in and then out again without a battle or a burning.

All through the month of August armed bands continued to patrol
the roads as a "scrub Congress," in the phrase of one scoffer, met at
Parkinson's Ferry, now Monongahela, to debate, pass resolutions
and move somewhat uncertainly toward separation from the United
States. Wild and ignorant rumors won belief. It was said that
Congress was extending the excise levy to plows at a dollar each, that
every wagon entering Philadelphia would be forced to pay a dollar,
that a tax was soon to be established at Pittsburgh of fifteen shillings
for the birth of every boy baby, and ten for each girl.

With the terrorizing of Pittsburgh, it was evident that the crisis
had arrived. The President requisitioned 15,000 militia from Pennsylvania, New Jersey, Virginia and Maryland, of whom about 13,000
actually marched. Would the citizens of one state invade another to
compel obedience to federal law? Here one gets a glimpse of the larger
importance of the affair. Both the national government and the state
of Pennsylvania sent commissioners to the West with offers of pardon
upon satisfactory assurances that the people would obey the laws.
Albert Gallatin, William Findley, Brackenridge and others made a
desperate effort to win the people to compliance, though their motives
were often questioned by both the rebels and the federal authorities.
The response to the offer of amnesty was judged not to be sufficiently
positive. Pressed by Hamilton to have federal power show its teeth,
Washington announced that the troops would march.

The army was aroused. In particular, the New Jersey militia were
ready for lynch law because they had been derided in a western newspaper as a "Water-mellon Army" and an uncomplimentary estimate
was made of their military capabilities. The piece was written as a
take-off on the kind of negotiations which preceded an Indian treaty.

Possibly the idea was suggested by the fact that the Whiskey Boys were often called "White Indians." At any rate, in the satire the Indians admonished the great council in Philadelphia: ". . . Brothers, we have that powerful monarch, Capt. Whiskey, to command us. By the power of his influence, and a love to *his person* we are compelled to every great and heroic act. . . . We, the Six United Nations of White Indians . . . have all imbibed his principles and passions— that is a love of whiskey. . . . Brothers, you must not think to frighten us with . . . infantry, cavalry and artillery, composed of your water-mellon armies from the Jersey shores; they would cut a much better figure in warring with the crabs and oysters about the Capes of Delaware."

Captain Whiskey was answered hotly by "A Jersey Blue." He pointed out that "the water-melon army of New Jersey" was going to march westward shortly with "ten-inch howitzers for throwing a species of mellon very useful for curing a *gravel occasioned by whiskey!*" The expedition was tagged thereafter as the "Watermelon Army."

The troops moved in two columns under the command of General Henry (Light Horse Harry) Lee, Governor of Virginia. Old Dan Morgan was there and young Meriwether Lewis, five nephews of President Washington, the governors of Pennsylvania and New Jersey, too, and many a veteran blooded in Revolutionary fighting, including the extraordinary German, Captain John Fries of the Bucks County militia and his remarkable dog to which the Captain gave the name of a beverage he occasionally enjoyed—Whiskey.

The left wing marched west during October, 1794, over General Braddock's old route from Virginia and Maryland to Cumberland on the Potomac, then northwest into Pennsylvania, to join forces with the right wing at Union Town. The Pennsylvania and New Jersey corps proceeded via Norristown and Reading to Harrisburg and Carlisle. There, on October 4th, President Washington arrived, accompanied by Colonel Hamilton. The representatives of the disaffected counties told the President at Carlisle that the army was not needed but Hamilton convinced him that it was. Washington proceeded with the troops as far as Bedford, then returned to Philadelphia for the meeting of Congress. Hamilton ordered a roundup of many of the rebels and personally interrogated the most important ones. Brackenridge, incidentally, came off well in his encounter with Hamilton, who declared that he was satisfied with Brackenridge's conduct.

By the time the expedition had crossed the mountains, the uprising was already coming apart at the seams. David Bradford, who had been excluded from the offer of amnesty, fled to Spanish Louisiana. About two thousand of the best riflemen in the West also left the country, including many a distiller, who loaded his pot still on a pack horse or a keel boat and sought asylum in Kentucky where, hopefully, a man could make "the creature" without giving the public debt a lift.

The punitive army moved forward in glorious autumn weather, raiding chicken coops, consuming prodigious quantities of the commodity which lay at the heart of the controversy. Richard Howell, governor of New Jersey and commander of the right wing, revived the spirits of the Jersey troops by composing a marching song, "Dash to the Mountains, Jersey Blue":

> To arms once more, our hero cries,
> Sedition lives and order dies;
> To peace and ease then did adieu
> And dash to the mountains, Jersey Blue.

Faded diaries, old letters and orderly books preserve something of the gala atmosphere of the expedition. At Trenton a Miss Forman and a Miss Milnor were most amiable. Newtown, Pennsylvania, was ticketed as a poor place for hay. At Potts Grove a captain of the cavalry troop got kicked in the shin by his horse. Among the Virginians, Meriwether Lewis enjoyed the martial excitement, wrote to his mother in high spirits of the "mountains of beef and oceans of Whiskey"; sent regards "to all the girls" and announced that he would bring "an Insergiant Girl to se them next fall bearing the title of Mrs. Lewis." If there was such a girl, he soon forgot her.

Yet where there is an army in being there are bound to be unpleasant occurrences. Men were lashed. Quartermasters stole government property. A soldier was ordered to put a Scotch-Irish rebel under guard. In execution of the order, he ran said insurgent through with his bayonet, of which the prisoner died. At Carlisle a dragoon's pistol went off and hit a countryman in the groin; he too died. On November 13, long remembered in many a cabin and stump-clearing as "the dis-

mal night," the Jersey horse captured various citizens whom they described grimly as "the whiskey pole gentry," dragging them out of bed,
tying them back to back. The troopers held their prisoners in a damp
cellar for twenty-four hours without food or water, before marching
them off at gun point to a collection center at Washington, Pennsylvania.

In late November, finding no one to fight, the army turned east
again, leaving a volunteer force under General Morgan to conciliate
and consolidate the position during the winter. Twenty "Yahoos" were
carried back to Philadelphia and were paraded by the Philadelphia
Horse through the streets of the city with placards marked "Insurrection" attached to their hats, in an odd federalist version of a Roman
triumph. The cavalry was composed, as an admirer said, of "young
men of the first property of the city," with beautiful mounts, uniforms
of the finest blue broadcloth. They held their swords elevated in the
right hand while the light flashed from their silver stirrups, martin-
gales and jingling bridles. Stretched over half a mile they came, first
two troopers abreast, then a pair of Yahoos, walking; then two more
mounted men, and so on.

The army, meditating upon their fatigues and hardships, called for
a substantial number of hangings. Samuel Hodgson, Commissary-
general of the army, wrote to a Pittsburgh confidant, "We all lament
that so few of the insurgents fell—such disorders can only be cured
by copious bleedings. . . ." Philip Freneau, friend and literary col-
league of Brackenridge, suggested in retrospect—ironically, of course
—the benefits which would have accrued to the country "If Washington had drawn and quartered thirty or forty of the whiskey boys. . . ."
Most of the captives escaped any punishment other than that of being
held in jail without a trial for ten or twelve months. One died. Two
were finally tried and sentenced to death. Eventually both were let off.

Gradually the bitterness receded. In August, 1794, General An-
thony Wayne had crushed the Indians at the Battle of Fallen Timbers.
A treaty was concluded with Spain in October, 1795, clearing the
Mississippi for western trade. The movement of the army into the
Pennsylvania hinterland, meanwhile, brought with it a flood of cash
which furnished the distillers with currency for paying their taxes.
These events served to produce a better feeling toward the Union.

If the rising was a failure, so was the liquor tax. The military adventure alone, without ordinary costs of collection, ran up a bill of $1,500,000, or about one third of all the money that was realized during the life of the revenue act. The excise was quietly repealed during Jefferson's administration. Yet the watermelon armies and the Whiskey Boys made a not inconsiderable contribution to our constitutional history. Through them, the year 1794 completed what 1787 had begun; for it established the reality of a federal union whose law was not a suggestion but a command.

II THE EMERGING REPUBLIC
1800–1877

Mr. Jefferson in 1801

MARSHALL SMELSER

• One of the most talented individuals ever to sit in the
White House, Thomas Jefferson is the only American President who may be classified as a truly Renaissance Man. Ex-
ceptionally gifted in a wide spectrum of activities, he not
only authored the Declaration of Independence and the
classic Notes on Virginia but also mastered Greek and Latin,
conversed in French and Italian, designed his own estate at
Monticello, became an accomplished horticulturist and violinist, founded the University of Virginia, and still made
time to participate dramatically in the politics of his era.
He distinguished himself as Governor of Virginia, as Ambas-
sador to France during the Confederation period, as George
Washington's first Secretary of State, as a founder of the
Democratic-Republican party, as a spokesman for individual
freedom in the Kentucky Resolutions of 1798, and of course
as President of the United States. In his inaugural address of
1801, he proclaimed "We are all Republicans, we are all
Federalists," but in his performance as President he displayed
a unique talent for mobilizing the members of his party into
a cohesive unit.

No American President has ever shown greater capacity
for altering previously enunciated views after entering the
White House. Despite his beliefs in strong local government,
state sponsorship of education, and rigid interpretation of
constitutional stipulations, as President he ran the country
with a hand more firm than that of any of his predecessors,
proposed that Congress support a national system of education, and interpreted the Constitution according to his own
goals. All in all Jefferson was a fascinating individual, and in
the following selection Marshall Smelser captures the man as
he appeared at the onset of his Presidential term.

From The Democratic Republic by Marshall Smelser. Copyright ©
1968 by Marshall Smelser. Reprinted by permission of Harper & Row,
Publishers, Inc.

At least we know what he looked like. He was tall and slender, framed of large, loosely shackled bones. His clothes, including a cherished scarlet vest and a pair of run-over slippers, never seemed quite to fit. He struck one observer as a man who was all ends and angles. A Federalist senator, William Plumer of New Hampshire, on calling at the White House, mistook him for "a servant" and carefully noted that he wore a dirty shirt. The senator was fair-minded enough to record the wearing of a clean shirt at a dinner some time later.

Mr. Jefferson's usual manner was good-humored, even sunny, although occasionally abstracted or cynical. His disposition fitted a country squire whose excellent health and enviable digestion gave him a lifelong euphoria, interrupted only by periodic headaches and occasional rheumatic twinges. He had the typical complexion of the freckled gray-eyed Celt. His hair was cut short and powdered. Its color we know, because a correspondent saluted him in a letter, carefully preserved by the recipient, as "You red-headed son of a bitch."

His small talk was built as loosely as his lounging body. Although often brilliant, his conversation was usually rambling and diffuse. It might range from weather and crops to the ingenuity of the Senate in finding excuses to recess during the local race meetings. Following the ponies was a lesser vice than dice; it gave the gentlemen "time for reflection," as he put it, between investments of their risk capital.

That was the exterior Jefferson as seen by the casual caller, but his personality had layers like an onion. His intimate friends knew the next layer, his family knew the third, but no one except God and Thomas Jefferson knew what lay farther inside this sensitive, unsentimental violinist, bird watcher, and horticulturist. We do know that forgiveness of his enemies did not come to him easily.

He broke the precedent of delivering messages orally to the Congress, which was set by George Washington and carried on by John Adams. Jefferson sent his messages to Capitol Hill to be read by a clerk. He said it was to save time, but we know he hated to speak in public, and he was only entirely at ease in the company of kinfolk, artists, savants, and a few Republican leaders. Margaret Bayard Smith, daughter of a warm Federalist and wife of the Republican editor of the new *National Intelligencer*, expected to meet a fanatical boor. To her surprise he was "so meek and mild, yet dignified in his manners, with a voice so soft and low, with a countenance so benignant and intelligent. . . ." But Anthony Merry, the British minister, and his wife did not think the President so dignified and benignant. When Jefferson, lacking a hostess, disregarded all protocol at state dinners, saying "pele-mele is our law," they felt literally degraded and quit coming to the White House. The Spanish minister joined the banquet boycott.

The absence of the diplomatic corps was not of first importance. To Jefferson the dinner party—particularly the stag dinner party— was a principal domestic political tool. Inviting not more than a dozen legislators at a time, he managed to get through the whole list more than once a session. The groups were chosen for compatibility. He seated them at a round table where he would be only first among equals and where private conversations would be difficult. He served his guests himself from a dumb-waiter to preclude the presence of eavesdropping servants. His French chef has been rated highly and his cellar must have been superb. Never dominating the conversation, he guided it away from the shoptalk in which congressmen found themselves already too much immersed, and planted the seeds of his political philosophy by indirection, letting his charm and his menu carry things along. The diplomatic corps knew well enough what he was doing, since it was the customary procedure of European courts, but to the political community in the raw new capital it seems to have been dazzling, and it showed Thomas Jefferson at his guileful best in the tactics of politics.

The contrast between his manner with Mrs. Smith across a tea table and his treatment of the diplomatic corps makes clear the split between his private life and his public bearing as the chief of state of a democratic republic. In private, the gentle introvert; in public matters, the incarnation of a stormy nation of freemen, willing to provoke contention, even though he found controversy painful. When relaxed with friends or family, his simple carriage was obviously not the way of a clod, but was more the manner of a negligent, self-assured nobleman, correctly confident of his status and of his own good taste. Yet, in a conference on the public's business, a senator could notice his "stiff gentility or lofty gravity."

It seems very unlikely that such an undramatic and diffident man, whose charm was felt only in private, could have reached the White House in any later generation. His merits were publicized only by his

friends. Not for him was the alley fighting of ballot politics. Once he
warned his grandson to avoid two kinds of disputants: self-assured
young intellectuals with more confidence than knowledge, and bad-
tempered, passionate politicians—these latter needed "medical more
than moral counsel."

Now peel down to the third layer. There one sees a homesick
widower with chronic money troubles, yearning for his children and
his grandchildren. His was a great career but rarely a happy life. Between 1772 and 1782, four of his six children died. In 1781 a British
army devastated his farm, and the difficulties of his term as governor
of Virginia left a faint smear on his reputation. Then in 1782 Mrs.
Jefferson died. At the age of forty his life had become a vacuum. It
is almost enough to explain his later career to say that political, scientific, and intellectual projects rushed into his vacant soul to fill that
vacuum and to make him the man we remember instead of the reclu-
sive squire he wished to be. His two surviving daughters married
young. One, Polly Jefferson Eppes, died in childbirth. He had a
brief hope of something approaching normal family life when both
of his sons-in-law were elected to the House of Representatives, but
each of the girls was advanced in pregnancy and dared not risk the
rigors of travel to Washington.

After assuming the debts of his father-in-law, his personal finances
were forever out of control. In old age he owed $107,000. When his
daughters married, there was nothing left for him to take pleasure in
except the talk of his intellectual friends, and the forty years of building and rebuilding Palladian Monticello. What he liked about Washington was that it lay between Monticello and "The American Philosophical Society Held at Philadelphia for the Diffusion of Useful
Knowledge."

II

All men claim to be Jeffersonians today. It is doubtful whether the
study of any other public man in our national story has been equally
absorbing to so many minds. Jefferson's popularity has reached its
zenith since 1920. The published evaluations differ so widely that
they tell us more about their writers than about Jefferson. There is
so much to see, so much to understand about this man of many
flashing facets that it requires more self-discipline than most students

have been willing to exercise in order to get the emphases in the right places. He would, perhaps, be easier to understand except for the monument of literary evidence he left us—fifty thousand items, dated from 1760 to 1826, one of the richest left by any man. It has not yet been completely mastered.

Thomas Jefferson's work has been scrutinized and searched not so much for understanding as to justify positions which often contradict each other. As the pendulum of public favor swings from generation to generation, he and Alexander Hamilton exchange the roles of Saint Michael and Lucifer. Laissez faire, states' rights, isolationism, agrarianism, rationalism, civil liberty, and constitutional democracy have all been fiercely defended by the use of quotations from Jefferson's writings, regardless of context. On a more sophisticated level of scholarship, professors drub each other with Jeffersonian tags to prove mutually exclusive generalizations. To get all of the academic theorizers under Jefferson's roof, we must label him the Agrarian Commercial Industrial Democratic Federalist. Fortunately for the history of the republic, the Jeffersonian administration, because of its optimistic evaluation of the public's common sense, was keen on explaining everything to the people. The wholly public business, despite the inner personal subtleties and complexities of the leaders, was very well documented, although one must read the public statements with the usual disciplined skepticism.

III

Nothing that promised the ultimate physical or moral improvement of mankind was alien to the polygonal mind of Thomas Jefferson. With the Adamses and Woodrow Wilson he was one of the four most intellectual of the Presidents of the United States, and he and Wilson are still the objects of hero worship by some Americans. His own heroes were Francis Bacon, Isaac Newton, and John Locke, a "trinity of the three greatest men the world had ever produced." His nominal occupations were farmer and lawyer. He was close to being a true scientist of agriculture, and he was a much more active and successful lawyer, at least up to 1771, when public affairs began to take more and more of his time, than has been generally known.

He mastered Greek and Latin before he was eighteen. Thereafter his reading revolved around the classical authors like a wheel around its hub. Because so few of us nowadays know the classics, we miss much in his mind. He not only knew Greek but he tried to reform its pronunciation by an essay in which he leaned more toward eighteenth-century Greek pronunciation than toward the Italian style then in vogue. He spoke French and Italian, although not fluently, and he had looked into, and had some acquaintance with, forty Indian languages. He also tried to reform the spelling of English. Although he was surely a first-rate writer of his own language, he thought of himself only as a discriminating reader. Omnivorous would be as good an adjective as discriminating. By 1794 he could honestly say he had the best library in the United States. Its 6,500 volumes, all of them collected since a fire destroyed his first library in 1770, formed the nucleus of the Library of Congress.

He must have been a pretty fair violinist or he could not have endured to practice as much as he did, and he certainly has won praise as an architect, but his attitude toward the arts was the attitude of his age. Artists were craftsmen who succeded if their works pleasantly filled the leisure of the connoisseur by giving him something animating, interesting, attractive to contemplate. Jefferson would not have understood the phrase "art for art's sake," nor could he have approved of the self-appointed Great Tormented Souls who floridly dominated the next generation's lush romanticism.

Thomas Jefferson was more inclined toward science than toward politics. He knew more of applied science, and he knew more scientists, than any of his American contemporaries. He was *the* American agricultural student of his day. For forty-seven years he belonged to the American Philosophical Society; for nearly twenty years he was its president and may have contributed more to its greatness than Benjamin Franklin. Not only was his *Notes on the State of Virginia* (1784–85) a respectable contribution, but his stimulation of the researches of other men, for example, Lewis and Clark, is an influence still felt. His scientific methods will still pass close scrutiny. If the Revolution had failed, and if he had escaped the gallows, he would probably have been barred from public life; in the seclusion of Albemarle County, Virginia, he likely would have become the father of American agricultural chemistry.

Early in life he lost his faith, but not his morals; nevertheless, he had his children baptized in the Anglican Church, attended Anglican services, and had all of his relatives buried according to the Anglican rites. In Pennsylvania, he was Unitarian; in Virginia, Episcopalian; and in the District of Columbia, who-knows-what. He ended as a deist after enduring a lifetime of fierce, intemperate, even slanderous attacks on his infidelity from many who became Unitarians, that is, deists, themselves. According to his home-made theology, Saint Paul corrupted Christianity to prove Christ divine. Better, he said, that men should apply reason to the Book of Nature in order to discover the laws of God.

This remarkable virtuoso, nationally honored for the virtues of the intellect before the time of the establishment of the federal government, was a talented connoisseur of all the arts. In some he had a taste and dexterity which approached professional standards. He was neither pure scientist nor pure philosopher.

IV

Thomas Jefferson's prefederal political career was the career of a man who hated contention, who was better at counsel than at execution, who was better in committee than on the floor. As the scribe of Independence he had drawn together the feelings of his fellow countrymen into superb but prudently circumscribed prose. He gained no glory as revolutionary governor of Virginia and, indeed, barely escaped the censure of the Virginia legislature at the end of his term. The famous legislative reforms in Virginia, which were enacted under his leadership, were merely reforms of the squirearchy.

His mild and conversationally uncontentious liberalism, and his diplomatic experience as minister to France, made him seem the natural choice for Secretary of State in President George Washington's new administration. Jefferson accepted the appointment reluctantly and assumed the office in March, 1790. At that moment in the story, the President and the Secretary were cordial friends, but their relations chilled in the late 1790's. When the new Secretary of State came to New York, he was walking on to a political battlefield. He did not take a place in the array immediately. Indeed, as late as 1792, he still recoiled from direct political action.

An opposition had emerged in the Congress, led by Representative James Madison of Virginia. It was hotly opposed to the Treasury policies of Alexander Hamilton. Madison and John Beckley, the Clerk of the House, carried the antiadministration banner. From early 1791 they had Jefferson's sympathy, but he did not create their faction. It recognized and claimed him as its leader. Not until 1796, during the fierce wrangle over the Jay Treaty, did Jefferson become the public partisan head of antifederalism. The notion that Jefferson founded the opposition was an invention of the Hamiltonians, to suit their short-range vote-getting purposes.

True, Jefferson disapproved of Hamilton's policies because Hamilton influenced the Congress to favor finance and commerce over farming. By late 1792 he was so stirred that he could describe Hamilton's career to the uneasy Washington as "a tissue of machinations against the liberty of the country," but the explanation of the history of the Federalist period as a struggle between Jefferson and Hamilton is useful only as what Broadus Mitchell called "a sociological shorthand." It was Madison and Beckley who organized the group that later made Jefferson its idol. The squire of Monticello has been sketched as a shadowy *provocateur* from 1790 to 1795, holding other men's coats while they smote the enemy in the public prints, but this picture too is a Hamiltonian caricature. Only twice did Jefferson urge men to take up their quills and stab Hamilton, and in each instance it was in a public debate on a question of deep importance. Jefferson was always available at the elbows of the front-rank anti-Hamiltonians, but he did not march in public. The famous liberal sentiments which are so venerated by modern democrats were—after 1776—all written in private letters, not for publication. Even during the campaign of 1800 he stayed at Monticello to supervise the baking of bricks, while letting his political views filter out to the public through letters to his friends.

Thomas Jefferson was never a flaming radical. His environment made it impossible, although there is a monumental Jeffersonian mythology which makes him out a doctrinaire democrat. In truth, he believed in getting what seemed best for the public good with as little painful acrimony and criticism as possible. He had no oratorical talent as a crowd pleaser and he never made a speech that brought cheers. The energy and admiration of his friends, not his own qualities of leadership, put him in the White House.

If the French Revolution had not caused a recanvass of fundamental libertarian principles, he and his supporters probably could not have

pulled off the electoral coup of 1800. Nor was his election a victory
for infidel rationalism. It was the counterattack of theologically conservative farmers against the Federalists' aristocratic contempt for
America's sunburned agricultural drudges. They thought they were
voting for electors, or assemblymen who would choose electors, who
would favor Thomas Jefferson, a Whiggish moderate, whose only controversial publications had been the Declaration of Independence and
the Virginia Statute for Religious Freedom long, long before. And
they were right.

V

Thomas Jefferson never wrote a formal comprehensive treatise of
political philosophy. His views were expressed in parts—in the Declaration of Independence, in his *Notes on Virginia*, his arguments
for legal reform in Virginia, the Kentucky Resolutions of 1798 (the
authorship of which was unknown when he was elected), inaugural
addresses, messages to the Congress, and, most of all, in private correspondence and conversation. Friends and enemies, with little public
help from him, pushed him forward to accept the Federalists' label
which tagged him as the chief symbol of opposition to Hamiltonian
Federalism. Liberty, not democracy, was the key word in his sometimes inconsistent political talk and correspondence.

When faced by a political problem, he went to printed classical
and modern sources for solutions which harmonized with his broad
political experience and observation. He can properly be called a
professional scholar of legal history and of the political history of
the seventeenth century, but his historical method was utilitarian
and servile. It was not used for pure understanding and liberal learning. Theoretical treatises which could not be applied immediately
to concrete and present questions had little appeal for him. His intellectual pedigree included the Epicureans; the Stoics; a purely human
Jesus Christ; John Locke; the Scottish common-sense philosophers;
Adam Smith; Henry St. John, Viscount Bolingbroke; Henry Home,
Lord Kames; and Dugald Stewart. Because the French *philosophes*
venerated some of the same masters, Jefferson was at ease when he
talked with them in France. In a sense, Jefferson's outlook in 1801
was reactionary. He consistently pressed for a return to the pure republicanism of the years of the American Revolution.

How much his mind owed to France is a fair question. His *Commonplace Book* shows his views were pretty well formed long before the French Revolution. The only French author who was extensively quoted in it was Charles Secondat de Montesquieu, but Jefferson only copied out the parts he already agreed with. No doubt his residence in France broadened his political outlook and, at the same time, stiffened his repugnance to monarchy, aristocracy, land monopoly, and urbanism. What he saw in France alerted him to the necessity for certain political safeguards to guarantee and to preserve agrarian republicanism. But he remained more Whig than *philosophe*.

Jefferson's faith in reason, education, and the future of America was fixed, but his procedures were adjustable. Unlike most of his contemporaries, he had a constitutional theory of change—"the earth," he said, "always belongs to the living." His political thought was a search for intellectual props for the democratic republican state. Such thinking is the method of an eclectic utilitarian rather than the method of a political philosopher. Because he was optimistically working for something new in the world's limitless future, his philosophical affirmations were necessarily a little indefinite. But certainly he was no doctrinaire. He studied history to learn the traps into which Great Britain had fallen. From his study he concluded that all had gone wrong since the Norman Conquest. Studying the age before the Norman Conquest, he thought he discovered an Anglo-Saxon utopia, an antifeudal utopia, which might be re-established in North America by directed progress toward the perfection of the past. Although he was a materialist in science, he accepted the notion of moral responsibility in man. Because he erroneously assumed that all men were as interested in public concerns as he was, he believed the United States could be as perfect as King Alfred's England, if every child were taught history as Thomas Jefferson understood it.

By a careful selection of his most liberal remarks, a specious case can be constructed to support a Jeffersonian anarchism, or something near it. The people, he said, if they had the proper education and the correct public information, were the only sure reliance for the preservation of liberty. A rebellion every twenty years might be a good thing. Constitutions and laws should periodically expire. "The tree of liberty must be refreshed from time to time with the blood of patriots and tyrants. It is it's [*sic*] natural manure." No men were congenitally of the governing or the governed classes. The Constitution must be changed only by amendment, not by interpretation. He even exceeded Locke in toleration, because he believed ridicule would kill opinions which were morally harmful to society. And, finally, there is the classic, much-quoted, but not authentic aphorism, "that government is best which governs least."

All of these politically relaxed apothegms can be matched by seemingly antagonistic opinions and legislative proposals: tax-supported schools, public libraries, and dispensaries, subsidized newspaper circulation, subdivision of great landholdings and the legal frustration of land speculators by geometrically proportional taxation, a literacy test for voting, a national transport system. He did not believe in simple, direct government, but wished for a sharp separation of powers and difficult methods of amending constitutions. Some of his views on the vigor of the powers of the President, written or spoken privately to George Washington during the 1790's, would have surprised his followers if they had been published.

The apparent paradox can be reconciled by remembering that liberty was his navigating star, even though there were cloudy nights in his career when he steered in another direction. He did not fear any act of the state except encroachment on civil liberty. Civil liberty comprised those rights guaranteed in the several American bills of rights which were drawn and ratified between 1776 and 1791. He would support any other use of that political power and authority which had been *delegated* by constitutional compact, if it seemed for the common good, and if it did not limit civil liberty. This liberalism had a strong agrarian color, which limits its relevance to the problems of a later industrial society. When he spoke of the people as the guardians of liberty, he meant farmers, who comprised nearly the whole people of the United States. City mobs were easily corruptible by largesse from the public funds. Land-owning farmers were unlikely to tax themselves in order to corrupt themselves. Like the several varieties of physiocrats, he opposed mercantilism, and his high opinion of Adam Smith's *Wealth of Nations*—"of money and commerce . . . the best book . . ."—suggests Smith as the source of his opposition. In sum, he thought if land were fairly distributed, and the business community (meaning the Federalists) could be prevented from manipulating the economy in its own interest, liberty was safe.

His thinking had already contributed to the form of the United States. His pamphlet *A Summary View* (1774) was among the first by a native American to forecast sharply the division of power and authority now found in our federal arrangement. By interpretation or misinterpretation, the implicit theory of state nullification of federal law, as written in his then anonymous "Kentucky Resolutions" of 1798, was to have catastrophic consequences long after his death. As a social-contract theorist, he believed the state of nature to be a state of peace. Applying this theory to international relations, he concluded that war was unnatural, peace natural. Therefore, he had sought and would continue to seek peace by every means possible.

Jefferson would have been more than human if he had always practiced what he preached. In private life he showed a certain meanness of spirit by carefully recording much of the derogatory gossip he heard about his political rivals and enemies, and having the manuscript bound as a literary monument to the difficulties of his cause. He also privately slandered his opponents by ungrounded accusations of monarchism. As a public official, at one time or other he supported or countenanced loyalty oaths for those of doubtful fidelity to the Revolution and internment camps for political suspects, drafted a bill of attainder, championed a peace process of outlawry (there being no process of extradition of fugitives), urged prosecutions for seditious libel, left himself open to charges of unconstitutional search and seizure, censored reading, and rated prospective professors according to their political orthodoxy. Of these lapses it can be said that they were in character for a man who so admired seventeenth-century Whiggery. He was never committed to the tyrannical side of his opponents, he aided the victory of liberty, and his abstract and formal teachings became the enduring positions while his concrete departures from his own principles were temporary.

On the immediate problems facing the union in the year of his inauguration as President, he appears to have joined with Edmund Pendleton and John Taylor of Caroline in a proposal to amend the federal Constitution (published in Richmond in October, 1801) which would have prohibited the re-election of the President, have given the Congress the appointment of judges and ambassadors, have shortened the terms of senators or have made them removable by their constituents, have prevented the appointment of judges and members of the Congress to other offices, have made judges removable by vote of the Congress, and have limited the federal borrowing power.

The proposals to "reform" the Constitution were not the proposals of the library politician. They were the reactions of Virginia Republicans as they looked back in anger at the Federalist policies which enacted the Hamiltonian fiscal program and the Alien and Sedition Acts. If the Republicans had remained in the minority for another decade or so, we would have heard more about these propositions.

VI

The lanky lord of Monticello came to Washington in November, 1800, to wait out the electoral vote. He called on John Adams and soothed the rude and angry loser, who wore his defeat like a knife in the ribs, by blaming the outcome of the election on the unpopularity of Adams' enemies in the Federalist party. Jefferson spent the winter in "Mayfair in the mud," which he had helped to lay out, as a lodger in Conrad and McMunn's boardinghouse—$15 a week, American Plan—where he modestly dined at the chilly foot of the long table, far from a seat of honor near the fire.

At noon on March 4, 1801, Jefferson took the oath of office in purposely, almost ostentatiously, simple circumstances intended to emphasize the Republican "revolution." He walked to the unfinished Capitol accompanied by two of Adams' cabinet officers, a handful of representatives, and a battery of Maryland militia gunners. In the Senate chamber he took his place with Vice-President Aaron Burr, the American Catiline who could never quite pull off any of his imperial schemes, and with cousin John Marshall, the Chief Justice and Jefferson's inveterate but honorable political foe. It was an interesting tableau. Each of the three men deeply distrusted the other two. There were two noticeable absences. John Adams had driven out of town into retirement by daybreak. Theodore Sedgwick, the arch-Federalist Speaker of the House, stayed away in fuming exasperation.

Probably no American presidential inaugural address has been heard by fewer people. The hall was packed, but Jefferson spoke his happily phrased remarks in a voice barely above a whisper. Perhaps only Marshall and Burr heard it all; however, printed copies were immediately distributed to the strained listeners.

The speech stated the Republican principles of that instant: justice for all, friendship with all nations and "entangling alliances with none," the support of state governments as "the surest bulwarks against antirepublican tendencies," the preservation of the strength of the union, "a jealous care of the right of election," majority rule, economy in government, individualism, payment of the public debts, "encouragement of agriculture and of commerce as its handmaid," dissemination of information, freedom of religion, press, and person. The cooled-off ex-democrat John Marshall must have winced internally at the President's remark, "I believe this . . . the strongest Government on earth," coming, as it did, from the apparent leader of antinationalism. Jefferson's assertion of majority rule was qualified by the requirement that minorities be protected by "equal laws," by which he no doubt meant laws in harmony with the Bill of Rights. The part assigned to the government in the economic order was the role of the referee who penalizes personal fouls—pretty much the Adam Smith view.

The most widely reprinted sentence of the speech was the famous remark, "We are all Republicans, we are all Federalists." His hatred of contention guarantees its sincerity, but it was politically dexterous to try to separate the rank and file of Federalists from their inept elder leaders. The "entangling alliances" phrase, which has been quoted almost as often, told all who cared to read between the lines that he accepted the abrogation of the French Alliance of 1778. These points were made especially to soothe the Federalists who were not irreconcilables. After all, Federalism still ruled New England, and it fought on even terms in New York. To anticipate a bit, Jefferson's tactics worked, as was proved in the series of elections which began in 1802.

Henry Adams, the most famous commentator on this day's work, saw Jefferson's ideal of the new republic of 1801 as "an enlarged Virginia"—agrarian, states'-rightist, frugal in government, strict constructionist, and hostile to the concentration of any kind of power in Washington, public or private. Virginia Republicanism was the most popular brand of republicanism; its only link with its northern allies was a "love of freedom." To which a latter-day commentator may presume to add that a love of freedom is a good first link for any alliance of Americans. In a letter acknowledging the congratulations of John Dickinson, Jefferson said the national "Argosy" had been

severely tested by a storm, but now, sailing on the "republican tack
. . . will show by the beauty of her motion the skill of her builders."
The storm he referred to was, of course, the great Jacobin scare of
the late 1790's which provoked the Federalists to attack civil liberty.
Now the gale had moderated. The ship of state was foaming through
a kindly sea.

On Inauguration Day, Thomas Jefferson dined as usual at Conrad
and McMunn's. When he entered the room, only one of his fellow
boarders, and that a lady, rose to offer him a chair. He declined her
invitation. In private life the foot of the table was good enough for
this President of the United States, although one cannot avoid notic-
ing also that this choice of seat was a very felicitous political gesture.

VII

Although some Republicans were pained by what seemed an appease-
ment of Federalism in the inaugural speech, William Branch Giles's
reaction, while somewhat overstated, was closer to being typical:
". . . the only American language I ever heard from the Presidential
chair."

Federalists were—shall we say?—less exhilarated, although Jefferson's moderation was a relief to John Marshall, the man who was to
be the most important Federalist in the decades to come. Equally
rational Federalists saw the President's subtlety in his appeal to their
followers, but decided to trust him until he proved himself unworthy.
However, the irreconcilables remained irreconcilables, making refer-
ences to the imminent smell of the "loathsome steam of human
victims offered in sacrifice" (Fisher Ames), and "that false, and flatu-
lent, and foolish paper" called the Declaration of Independence
(Joseph Dennie). In public, Alexander Hamilton pretended to be
pleased at Jefferson's conversion to Federalism; in private, he was
disgusted at the ease of the seduction of rank-and-file Federalists—
and even of some of the second-level leaders. President Timothy
Dwight sat stoutly intransigent in his study at Yale. To him, Thomas
Jefferson was only the latest in an infamous line of false prophets,
standing in a file which stretched back for centuries. In *An Oration*,
at Hartford in July, 1801, he foresaw a "country governed by block-
heads and knaves . . . the ties of marriage . . . severed; our wives
and daughters thrown into the stews. . . ." Poor Dwight was living

through the decay of the New England religious establishment. Thomas Jefferson, the personal devil whose fault it was, might be exorcised by speeches intended to arouse the Federalist church militant to its early flame. Dwight wasted his breath. Jefferson's election had no visible religious consequences. Instead, it was immediately followed by a great fundamentalist religious revival which probably affected far more Jeffersonian voters than Federalist. The intransigents would have been wiser to fear Jefferson's understanding, imagination, and unconsciousness of his rank, for those were the qualities which made him dangerous to Federalism. Federalism was long on intelligence and administrative ability, but short on more popular qualities.

A good many irreconcilable Federalists, mostly older men, withdrew from public life in the years immediately after Jefferson's first inauguration, weakening their group, which already had too many members who felt that practical politics was beneath the dignity of true gentlemen. Younger Federalists, less queasy, complained of the retreat, but many elders had become convinced that the avenues to public life were now dishonorable. Some, however, did not abandon the field entirely, but spent their energy entirely in local politics. In the years of the first blossom of Democratic-Republican triumph, only Hamilton, of all front-rank Federalist national leaders, had a national battle plan. In 1802, he privately proposed to James A. Bayard of Delaware the formation of a Christian Constitutional Society as what we would now call a front organization. It would function to disseminate information by correspondence, to promote candidates by the same means, and to carry out works of mercy for the relief of immigrants and the education of workingmen. But Bayard thought it unnecessary because, in his opinion, the Democratic-Republicans would destroy their popularity by their blunders.

The Federalists were melancholy in 1801, and well they might be, for they would never again capture the Capitol or the White House. They had made the republic a success, but they had also made the mistake of letting the people know they thought the people unfit to govern. Jefferson, the demon sent to buffet them, identified himself with causes, as Dumas Malone well said, "for which time was fighting." He was sensitive to fluctuations in the public will. Carefully obscuring his views from the public eye, he worked through other men. From him they received encouragement and inspiration. From them he got devotion and election to the Presidency. All things considered, he was a more representative American than any of his enemies.

It is surprising to reflect on what few hard facts the public, at home or abroad, knew about Jefferson on his Inauguration Day. Federalist ferocity had built him up as the principal foe of the Hamiltonian design, and, unwittingly, as a symbol of liberty and of American-style egalitarianism. His election was not the upthrusting of a personally known and beloved leader. Jefferson's election was, instead, the repudiation of Federalist disdain for the people.

The West and the American Age of Exploration

WILLIAM H. GOETZMANN

• In the 1960's one American in every five moved to a new home every year, a statistic often used to document the high degree of residential mobility in contemporary American society. But the United States has seemed always to be a nation on the move. In the 1830's the celebrated French visitor Alexis de Tocqueville wrote:

> . . . a man builds a house in which to spend his old age, and he sells it before the roof is on; . . . he brings a field into tillage, and leaves other men to gather the crops, he embraces a profession and gives it up; he settles a place, which he soon afterwards leaves, to carry his changeable longings elsewhere.

It is tempting to speak of this obsession with change and impatience with delay as the result of the geographical vastness of the United States. In the following essay, however, Professor William H. Goetzmann of the University of Texas studies several aspects of our culture to present a different perspective on the age of exploration. He argues that "westering" was part of a larger world-wide impulse, and he suggests that the American West had a powerful influence upon the East as well as the frontier.

Of all the major events in American history, none has been so central as the experience of the westward movement. The story of the confrontation and eventual domination of the vast empty continent by successive waves of pioneer Americans has become our national epic. This epic was most clearly articulated by the historian Frederick Jack-

From *Arizona and the West*, 2 (1960), 265–78. Reprinted by permission of *Arizona and the West*.

son Turner in his celebrated hypothesis on the significance of the
frontier in American history. "Stand at Cumberland Gap," he declared, "and watch the procession of civilization marching single file
—the buffalo following the trail to the salt springs, the Indian, the fur
trader and hunter, the pioneer farmer—and the frontier has passed by.
Stand at South Pass in the Rockies a century later and see the same
procession with wider intervals between." For Turner, and for those
who have followed after him in the celebration of his American myth,
it was the frontier which focused American energies; and it was the
West as the place—wild, isolated, and infinitely challenging—which
formed that peculiarly adventurous democrat, the American. Turner
asserted:

> This perennial rebirth, this fluidity of American life, this expan-
> sion westward with its new opportunities, its continuous touch
> with the simplicity of primitive society, furnish the forces domi-
> nating American character. The true point of view in the history
> of this nation is not the Atlantic Coast, it is the Great West.

Historians and poets of the West, taking their cue from Turner,
have turned their backs upon the Atlantic Coast, and have looked at
the great national experience as something Western—peculiarly Western. Indeed the very opposition between the Atlantic Coast and the
Great West—between the rimland and the heartland, the old and
wicked and the new and hopeful, as it were—has become a part of
this national story. The westward movement of the American people
has always been considered peculiarly "Western," and to suggest that
it was anything else has been to taint somehow the pristine American-
ness of the whole fable. The study of the westward movement is the
study of what happened in the West and nothing else; unless, of
course, one were to suggest that experiences in the West had great
impact upon the rest of the country.

It has always been permissible, of course, for the Western historian
to say with Turner, that "to the frontier the American intellect owes
its striking characteristics." But perhaps in celebrating and studying
the great story of the westward movement the Western historian has
taken too narrow a view. Perhaps he has really been guilty of under-
estimating the extent of this impulse to move into the unknown and

uncharted wildernesses of the world. Might it not be possible that this experience in the American West was an experience that was characteristic of the whole of America rather than just a part of it? Indeed, there is reason to suspect that the impulse for expansion over the globe might even be as characteristic of European civilization as a whole as it was for those hardy pioneers way out West. It might even be that one of the reasons for the enthusiastic acceptance of the myth of the American West was its very centrality to the whole of American experience at that particular time and place in the nineteenth century, and perhaps even today.

The recent interest in cultural history, and the corresponding use of new source materials, has begun to afford the historian new points of view toward all aspects of American history. Increasing importance has been attached to the cultural settings of well-known political events, and the historian has become more conscious of American behavioral patterns as they exist within the whole context of modern European experience. A recent example of this is Walter Prescott Webb's *The Great Frontier,* which takes a long view of the American frontier experience and designates to it a relatively small place in the course of the great 400-year boom which he declares has characterized European development since 1500. Inaccurate though his work might be in detail and in some of the conclusions he draws, nevertheless Professor Webb's thesis must stand as a significant attempt to break free of traditional approaches to the American West which have been dominated too much by nationalism and emphasis upon internal political events. If it does nothing else, Professor Webb's thesis at least has the advantage of suggesting a new dimension for the expansion impulse and a new set of kinship relationships which extend to all parts of our common culture.

The purpose here is a similar one. Let us abandon for the moment the traditional narrow view of the expansion impulse and take up another point of view. Let us focus upon the history of exploration in the American West as part of the general history of American and European culture between the years 1800 and 1860, a quite arbitrary time span but one that is central to the course of American westward expansion. In this period public enthusiasm for the discovery and exploration of exotic places reached a culmination due to the impetus of the romantic imagination and the rapid development of scientific techniques. So widespread was such enthusiasm that one might almost be justified in calling this sixty-year period "The American Age of Exploration." The keynote of this public enthusiasm was struck on Columbus Day, 1855, in the Washington *National Intelligencer*:

> The present is emphatically the age of discovery. At no period since the days of Columbus and Cortez has the thirst for exploration been more active and universal than now. One by one the outposts of barbarism are stormed and carried, advanced parallels are thrown up, and the besieging lines of knowledge, which when once established can never be retaken, are gradually closing around the yet unconquered mysteries of the globe. Modern exploration is intelligent, and its results are therefore positive and permanent. The traveller no longer wanders bewildered in a cloud of fables prepared to see marvels, and but too ready to create them. He tests every step of his way by the sure light of science and his pioneer trail becomes a plain and easy path to those who follow. The pencil, the compass, the barometer, and the sextant are his aids; and by these helps his single brain achieves results now which it would once have required an armed force to win.

The *Intelligencer* was not referring solely to American exploration but to activity by Americans and Europeans all over the globe. Stimulated by the eighteenth-century voyages of Captain Cook, the daring adventures of Alexander McKenzie, and the exotic excursions of Alexander von Humboldt into the green world of the Amazon Basin, Europeans and Americans alike increasingly began to undertake important expeditions—with the result that by about 1900 virtually all the interiors of the great continents had been explored, the sea lanes charted, and the Arctic and Antarctic discovered and to some extent explored.

Humboldt was a key figure of the period not only because of his work in South and Central America, but because somehow he combined the cosmopolitan rationalism of the eighteenth century with the newer romantic feeling for the grandeur and exoticism of nature into a scientific approach that could be understood and imitated by those who came after him. His purpose was a clear as any in that time of romantic strivings. From his field headquarters in the heart of the Andes he wrote:

> The ultimate aim of physical geography is . . . to recognize
> unity in the vast diversity of phenomena. . . . I have conceived
> the mad notion of presenting, in a graphic and attractive man-
> ner, the whole of the physical aspect of the universe in one work,
> which is to include all that is at present known of celestial and
> terrestrial phenomena, from the nature of the nebula down to
> the geography of the mosses clinging to a granite rock. . . .

Throughout the period he remained a kind of spiritual godfather and
grand advisor to great numbers of American and European scientists
and explorers. His influence on American explorers of the early West,
for example, is clearly indicated by the fact that his name even today
is attached to such prominent geographical features as the Humboldt
Range and the Humboldt River.

At the outset certain geographical areas and problems were of special interest to various nations. Since Napoleon's campaigns in Egypt,
French, British, and German explorers roamed over the continent of
Africa in increasing numbers, searching for everything from gorillas
to the source of the Nile. Men like Speke, Burton, du Chaillu, Krapf,
and Livingstone were heroes of the hour as they searched out the secrets of the dark continent. In North America the central focus was for
a long time upon the discovery of a Northwest Passage, or at least a
satisfactory trade route to India. McKenzie's great Canadian explorations had not entirely solved this problem, and it was not until Lewis
and Clark marched down the Columbia to the Pacific, that any satisfactory answer was forthcoming. National rivalries over the priority of
discoveries developed a particular intensity, not only in North America
and Africa, but even in such remote areas as the Antarctic where Europeans and Americans hotly contested the honor of discovering the new
continent—even to the extent of warping the viewpoints of old and
established learned societies. And all the while they remained virtually
ignorant of its prior discovery by commercial sealers from Stonington,
Connecticut, some twenty years before.

Although these various expeditions throughout the world were based
to a large extent upon the exigencies of national economic and political considerations, they were motivated also by an insatiable scientific curiosity. Most of the explorers seemed bent on collecting, ex-
amining, and classifying all of the various phenomena of nature which,

in and of itself, seemed a vast and infinitely mysterious thing. Darwin's voyage on the *Beagle* (1832–36), inspired by the work of Humboldt, is an outstanding example of such intellectual activity.

In all of this furious activity the young republic of the United States played an important part. Under the guidance of Thomas Jefferson, Americans turned after 1800 to the task of exploring the Great West. Official expeditions were sent out under Lewis and Clark, Dunbar and Hunter, Dunbar and Freeman, Pike, and Stephen H. Long. Private John Colter of the United States Army, on detached duty from the Lewis and Clark Expedition, became the first American to see the marvels of Yellowstone Park. It was Jefferson who played the key role not only in the planning of the expeditions but in devising a proper way to present the projects to an economy-minded Congress little interested at the time in the possible contributions of "pure science." Invariably these expeditions were presented to Congress as economic and political necessities, with their scientific objectives appearing to be an afterthought.

In considering the total picture of American achievement in exploration it would, of course, be a serious mistake to overlook the private interests that accomplished so much between 1806 and 1842. The mountain men, in particular, formed one of the most spectacular groups of explorers in all history as they roamed free and unrestrained (except by the Indians) all over the western half of North America. Jim Bridger, Jedediah Smith, and James Pattie were among the first Americans to see such geographical landmarks as the South Pass, the Great Basin, the Great Salt Lake, and the Grand Canyon. Fur magnates like John Jacob Astor, Pierre Chouteau, William H. Ashley, and Charles Bent, sponsored expeditions of their own which searched out the hitherto secret places of the West. On numerous occasions they afforded opportunities for savants, like the botanist Thomas Nuttall, or the geographer Joseph Nicollet, to extend their researches into the West.

By 1842, however, the day of the mountain man was about at an end, and in that year Jim Bridger settled down to the life of a trader in his fort at the South Pass in the Rockies. Then a new era began, one that was dominated by the United States Army's Topographical Engineers, of which the most representative figure was the boyish hero

John C. Fremont. Fremont's expeditions to the Far West in 1842, '43, '44, and '45 are all well known, but less well known are the exploits of his colleagues in the Corps of Topographical Engineers. Unlike the mountain men, these new explorers were interested in mapping the West and making its resources known to the generations of pioneers that would follow them. For the most part the Topographical Engineers considered themselves men of science, and they rarely failed to utilize the opportunities afforded them by their Western expeditions to record and publish their scientific data to the world.

During the Mexican War Lieutenants William H. Emory and James W. Abert explored and mapped the Southwest, calling the attention of scholars to the importance of the pueblos and other evidences of vanished Indian civilizations. Later Captain Lorenzo Sitgreaves and Lieutenant James Hervey Simpson explored the pueblo country of Arizona and New Mexico more closely, and together with Emory and Abert they were instrumental in launching the study of archaeology in the Southwest with reports on such important sites as the Chaco and Chelly Canyons and the Casa Grande on the Gila River. Captain Howard Stansbury and his assistant, Lieutenant John W. Gunnison, made the first scientific map of the Great Salt Lake in 1850, and Stansbury explored the western edge of the Lake for the first time. Captain John N. Macomb picked his way through the incredibly difficult country along the San Juan River to the junction of the Green and Grand Rivers, and thus became the first American to thoroughly understand the broad outlines of the Colorado River system. Lieutenant Joseph Christmas Ives chugged up the Colorado River in a homemade steamboat and led a party on foot to the floor of the Grand Canyon for the first time. This was a sublime moment in the history of Western exploration. Captain Randolph Barnes Marcy discovered the long elusive sources of the Red River in the Palo Duro Canyon of the Staked Plains of West Texas. Other Army explorers mapped the Great Basin and the Upper Missouri-Yellowstone River Country.

When these Army officers returned to make their findings known, they were assisted by the leading scientific men in the country—men like John Torrey, Asa Gray, James Hall, John Strong Newberry, and Louis Agassiz. F. V. Hayden's work with Lieutenant G. K. Warren

in the Dakotas helped to launch the serious study of vertebrate pale-
ontology in the United States. Some of the scientists who accompanied
the expeditions were so enthusiastic in the pursuit of knowledge that
they even attempted to pickle some of the Indians and bring them
back to the Smithsonian in a jar!

The outstanding publications of this period of military exploration
in the West were the Mexican Boundary Survey report and the report on the surveys for the Pacific Railroad. The Boundary Survey
report, in three massive volumes, constituted a matchless compendium
of information on the Southwest, particularly in the fields of geology,
botany and zoology. The Pacific Railroad reports were published in
thirteen volumes between 1853 and 1859, and these also included
monumental data on bird, fishes, mammals, plants and geology. The
most important contribution of the Pacific Railroad reports, however,
was Lieutenant G. K. Warren's master map of the whole trans-
Mississippi West published in 1857. It presented for the first time a
reasonably accurate and scientific outline of the whole country west
of the Mississippi, and it was a climactic event in the history of Western exploration.

The maps, the reports, the illustrations, the scientific data, and
most of all the accounts of the expeditions themselves all added up
to a picture of the American West as a vast and exotic place—a land
of gigantic sunless canyons, towering mountains, burning lakes and
fountains, mud-daubed Indians who lived in sky-high palaces, locust-
eaters scarcely out of the Stone Age, immense herds of buffalo stretch-
ing for miles over the limitless horizon—all virtually untouched by
the hand of civilization. And though these reports were intended as
scientific documents, they helped to set the tone of an age devoted
to exploration and the romantic desire to see ever outward from the
immediate circle of one's own existence to the remote frontiers of
the universe, just as Humboldt had dreamed of being the single genius
who would capture all knowledge of the cosmos in one massive compendium. This compulsion, as much as the often-stressed desire for
free land, drove the spearhead of American civilization into the West
during the so-called period of Manifest Destiny.

This aspect of Manifest Destiny, however, was not confined solely
to the desire to explore the Western land frontier. While most of the

agrarian states were urging Federal sponsorship of Western surveys, maritime interests on the Eastern seaboard and professional scientists in Washington saw to the launching of naval expeditions to all parts of the world, some of them with the admitted purpose of maintaining the national prestige in competition with the other nations bent on exploring and subduing the globe. The first of these expeditions was conceived by John Quincy Adams, the most scientifically-inclined of American presidents. He had proposed, during his presidency, a naval expedition to the Northwest Coast that would not only collect scientific data but would also be of direct assistance to American maritime interests in whaling and trading. His plan would complete the much desired passage to India. The plan, however, languished during the administration of Andrew Jackson. Finally in 1838 the United States Exploring Expedition, commanded by Lieutenant Charles Wilkes, set sail for the Pacific by way of South America and Cape Horn. This expedition, the most spectacular of its day, was gone for four years during which time it made scientific surveys and collections in South America, re-discovered the Antarctic Continent, charted its coast, made extensive explorations in the South Seas and Polynesian Islands, and cruised along the Northwest Coast of North America where a short party mapped much of what is now Washington and Oregon. Although the expedition included only one first-rate scientist, James Dwight Dana, it still contributed a great deal to science in the form of maps and collections.

South America proved irresistible to Navy explorers. Like the Portuguese adventurers of the fifteenth century they sailed southward in a series of expeditions designed partially to secure scientific information, but primarily to open up a vast new continent to commercial exploitation. The most sincerely scientific American expedition was Lieutenant James Melville Gilliss's astronomical expedition to Chili in 1849–50. Gilliss's chief objective was to measure the distance of the sun from the earth by making an observation of the planet Venus at a time when it was being observed by astronomers at the Naval Observatory in Washington. This part of his plan was frustrated, however, when officials at the Naval Observatory failed to carry out their part of the operation. Other expeditions sent to South America by the Navy included Lieutenant Page's expedition to the Rio De La

Plata in 1853–56, Lieutenant Michler's Atrato expedition, a joint Army-Navy venture to reconnoiter for an isthmian canal, and the spectacular exploration of the Amazon and Orinoco rivers by Lieutenant William L. Herndon and Midshipman Lardner Gibbon. This latter expedition was sent out purposely to survey the possibilities of the Amazon Basin for the establishment of a future slave empire when the South might be forced to give up its slaves due to Northern pressure. It was inspired by an arch-Southerner, Lieutenant Matthew Fontaine Maury, commander of the Naval Observatory in Washington and unofficial "Prince Henry the Navigator" to the American maritime expeditions of the whole period.

The Herndon and Gibbon expedition inflamed the imagination of the whole country. Upon reading of it in 1853, young Sam Clemens quit his newspaper job and started down the Mississippi, determined to be a coffee planter in Brazil. It was only a lack of funds that prevented him from reaching the Amazon, and turned him instead to the profession of Mississippi riverboat pilot. A few years later Frederick Church, a young Connecticut painter, also inspired by his reading of Humboldt and Herndon, actually made the journey to South America, where he recorded on canvas the grandeur and sublimity so often felt by the explorers.

Maury, as head of the Naval Observatory, served the cause of exploration in still another important way. He devised a system of logbooks to be carried by every merchant and whaling ship. These logbooks were forwarded to Washington and used by Maury to complete his important *Wind and Current Charts*, which amounted to a unique and accurate geography of the ocean. This project, along with his significant volume of *Sailing Directions*, has caused Maury to be regarded as a pioneer of the modern science of oceanography. His work also had the immense practical consequence of cutting the sailing time from New York to San Francisco by forty-seven days at a time when eager gold seekers had every reason to be eternally grateful.

Other naval expeditions of the period included Matthew Perry's voyage to Japan, Ringgold and Rodgers' North Pacific Exploring Expedition, and Elisha Kent Kane's voyage to the Arctic in search of the lost British explorer, Sir John Franklin. At the same time, too, Lieutenant Lynch was sent on a special mission to explore the Dead

Sea and parts of the West Coast of Africa. Thus, taken as a while, there was a considerable amount of official maritime exploration during the entire period. The official exploration was matched on sea as it was on land by the numerous private expeditions of whalers, sealers, and merchant adventurers. Any account of maritime exploration in this period can no more afford to ignore these than can the historian of the West afford to leave out the mountain men.

One further form of exploration during this period was the semi-private expedition in which a man received a governmental post which sent him to the place where he could do the exploring that he desired. The most notable examples of this were John Lloyd Stephens and Ephraim George Squier, who were sent to Central America on diplomatic missions so that they might explore the jungle regions. Stephens produced the monumental *Incidents of Travel in Central America, Chiapas, and Yucatan* which, with its magnificent illustrations executed by Frederick Catherwood, gave the first clear picture of the lost civilization of the Mayas. Squier also produced some highly important archaeological works on Central America.

Most of these men belonged to a curious literary group, interested in travel books, which met at Bartlett and Welford's bookstore in New York's Astor Hotel. The patriarch of the group was the aged Albert Gallatin; it also included such figures as Dr. F. S. Hawks, William Kennedy, George Folsom, and Brantz Mayer, author of *Mexico As It Is and As It Was*. On occasion, Edgar Allan Poe dropped in for meetings and gathered material for his own fictionalized versions of the travel book. The guiding spirit of the group was John Russell Bartlett, who got himself made United States-Mexican Boundary Commissioner in 1852 so that he could go to the Southwest and write a sequel to Stephens' enormously successful work on the Mayas. Bartlett proved to be a colossal failure as Boundary Commissioner; but he produced still another interesting travel book, his *Personal Narrative of Exploration in Texas, New Mexico, California, Sonora, and Chihuahua*, which is one of the most delightful books in the entire literature of the American West.

In general these men produced works on the borderline between serious science and romantic travel literature in which the strange and the exotic were the most important objectives. As it was for Humboldt himself, it was quite difficult for them to separate the two because the main impetus for scientific investigation seems to have been generated by the romantic interest in the unique and the marvelous—in the minutiae of nature as well as in the extremities of the cosmos—that hung over and dominated the entire period.

Much of the literature of the day contributed to and drew inspiration from this spirit, suggesting that it was all part of an imaginative whole. Books like Francis Parkman's *Oregon Trail* or Washington Irving's *Astoria & the Adventures of Captain Bonneville* were romanticized chronicles that nevertheless also contributed factual information about the West at a time when such information was sorely needed. *The Adventures of James Ohio Pattie*, Lewis H. Garrard's *Wah-to-Yah and the Taos Trail*, and Josiah Gregg's *Commerce of the Prairies* all belong in this category. They conveyed much useful data about the West; but their chief significance was that they presented a picture of the West as an exotic unknown, a place of adventure for the man of spirit and daring to go and make his mark. In the 1840's and '50's the West was our Africa, or Polynesia, or the Road to Xanadu. Yet the majority of serious economic and political historians tend to take this for granted—if they do not scorn it entirely as a motive for moving West. The color and spirit of the West have been left to Hollywood, as if it never really did matter as an operative force which spurred people westward. But surely such a spirit played its part in the settlement of Western America and should not be overlooked. It was an integral part of the age.

It is relatively easy, for example, to trace the impact of the whole age of exploration upon imaginative and popular literature. Cooper used Sir John Franklin's expedition as source material for the *Sea Lions*, the Wilkes Expedition for the *Crater*, and the Long Expedition for the *Prairie*. Poe, always a devotee of romantic science, used the theory of Semmes Hole as the basis for his *MS. Found in a Bottle* and the *Narrative of A. Gordon Pym*. His work, usually regarded as science fiction, was actually more closely attuned to the age of exploration than it was to pure science. Indeed every major writer of the period was touched to some extent in plot, character, and imagery by the spirit of exploration. Melville was, of course, in *Typee*, so carefully researched, and in *Moby Dick* and *Mardi* and virtually all the

rest of his work. Hawthorne had a fling at the travel book in his
Marble Faun, and he too was swayed by the exotic. Emerson was devoted to Humboldt; and Thoreau, his friend, always traveled West in
spirit from Walden Pond. Walt Whitman epitomizes the entire complex of travel, and the romantic exploration of the open road, with
his endless catalogues celebrating everything in nature. He was likewise
enamored with the idea of the West and the passage to India.

If we put all of these aspects of American culture together—the
scientific, the literary, the impact of the frontier, the rational techniques and the romantic enthusiasms—we get a somewhat different
perspective on this period of American history. What was happening
on the trans-Mississippi frontier was akin to the activities on the Eastern seaboard. The drive for maritime expansion, as Professor Norman
Graebner has recently pointed out, had as much to do with the course
of Manifest Destiny as the desire for free land. All aspects of American expansionism were to some extent part of a larger impulse which
was world-wide and extremely competitive. Intellectually, this might
be explained by the fact that at this moment the scientific and rational mind of the eighteenth century was exposed to a true world
horizon—and, as that mind went to work in the effort of compre-
hension, it became romantic. Whatever was but dimly known became
irresistibly attractive, and it was this attraction itself that had much
to do with stimulating the impulse of Manifest Destiny on a global
basis.

Viewed in this way, the experience in the American West seems
somewhat less than unique. Rather it appears as a part of a much
larger whole—a great synthesis which extends all the way from the
picturesque trappers' rendezvous in Cache Valley to the dimly lit
study of Humboldt in Potsdam. When we have worked long enough
and hard enough at studying this whole complex of ideas and emotions, we may perhaps arrive at a different view of our national and
international history in which the old concepts will have been given
a new and richer dimension. With particular regard to our own American West, we will have broken away from the old Turnerean tyranny
which has failed to satisfy us for a number of years but which is still
too valuable emotionally to part with completely. We will then be
closer to understanding what the old Westerner meant when he said:

It wasn't Indians that were important, nor adventures, nor even getting out here. It was a whole bunch of people made into one big crawling beast. . . . It was westering and westering. Every man wanted something for himself, but the big beast that was all of us wanted only westering. . . . It wasn't getting out here that mattered, it was movement and westering.

The Ideology of American Expansion

JULIUS PRATT

• American foreign policy in both the nineteenth and twentieth centuries has been rooted in two cardinal beliefs: the Monroe Doctrine and Manifest Destiny. Indicating that the United States would consider it a threat to herself if any European nation attempted to gain a foothold in this hemisphere, President James Monroe's message to Congress in 1823 has been sanctioned by most Americans as having the effect of an international law. The other doctrine that God has chosen us to do His will on earth is also a basic tenet of American policy. Whether we moved westward, freed the Cubans from Spanish tyranny in 1898, took over the Philippines, entered World War I to make the world safe for democracy, or acted as leader of the "free world" to thwart Communist expansion, American policymakers have justified their actions in moral terms. In 1968 when the late Robert F. Kennedy announced his entry into the competition for the Democratic Presidential nomination, his speech included the statement: "At stake is not simply the leadership of our party and even our country, it is our right to the moral leadership of this planet." When one recognizes that a belief in moral superiority and our right to leadership are essentially the guiding forces behind the actions of the American Presidents, one can understand why the United States acts as it does in foreign affairs.

In the following selection Julius Pratt elaborates upon these ideas and explains how the American government has justified its territorial acquisitions.

From *Essays in Honor of William E. Dodd*, ed. by A. Craven, Chicago: University of Chicago Press, 1935. Copyright © 1935 by the University of Chicago Press. Reprinted by permission.

Lincoln Steffens has observed that Americans have never learned to do wrong knowingly; that whenever they compromise with principle or abandon it, they invariably find a pious justification for their action. One is reminded of this observation in reviewing the history of American territorial expansion. For every step in that process, ingenious minds have found the best of reasons. From the year 1620, when King James the First granted to the Council for New England certain "large and goodlye Territoryes" in order "to second and followe God's sacred Will," to the year 1898, when William McKinley alleged that he had divine sanction for taking the Philippine Islands, it has been found possible to fit each successive acquisition of territory into the pattern of things decreed by divine will or inescapable destiny. The avowal of need or greed, coupled with power to take, has never satisfied our national conscience. We needed Florida and the mouth of the Mississippi; we thought we needed Canada, Texas, Oregon, California. But when we took, or attempted to take, that which we needed, we persuaded ourselves that we were but fulfilling the designs of Providence or the laws of Nature. If some of the apologists for later ventures in expansion were more frank in avowing motives of "national interest," the pious or fatalistic justification was none the less present.

The idea of a destiny which presides over and guides American expansion has rarely, if ever, been absent from the national consciousness. The precise character of that destiny, however, as well as the ultimate goal to which it points, has varied with changing ideas and circumstances. One of its earliest forms was geographical determinism. Certain contiguous areas were thought of as surely destined for annexation because their location made them naturally part of the United States. This idea seems to have been the basis for Thomas Jefferson's sure conviction that Florida would inevitably become American territory. In this expectation his mind never wavered; he questioned only the time and the means. The settling of Americans in Florida, he wrote in 1791, "will be the means of delivering to us peaceably, what may otherwise cost us a war." The failure of his own efforts to secure it did not shake his faith. In 1820, when it appeared likely that Spain would not ratify the Florida-purchase treaty, he wrote Monroe that this was not to be regretted. "Florida," he said, ". . . is ours. Every nation in Europe considers it such a right. We need not care for its occupation in time of peace, and, in war, the first cannon makes it ours without offence to anybody." Jefferson's belief was widely shared. Florida, said *Niles' Register* in 1819, "will just as naturally come into our possession as the waters of the Mississippi seek the sea; . . . We believe this is the universal conclusion of the United States. . . ." The young expansionists who led the country into war in 1812 in the hope of conquering Canada and Florida appealed to the God of Nature in behalf of their plans. "In point of territorial limit, the map will prove its importance," one of them proclaimed. "The waters of the St. Lawrence and the Mississippi interlock in a number of places, and the great Disposer of Human Events intended those two rivers should belong to the same people"; while to another it appeared that "the Author of Nature has marked our limits in the south, by the Gulf of Mexico; and on the north, by the regions of eternal frost." If neither of these Congressmen was able to discern the westward limits set by the Author of Nature, this task was performed by a writer for a south-western paper, who asked rhetorically: "Where is it written in the book of fate that the American republic shall not stretch her limits from the capes of the Chesapeake to Nootka sound, from the isthmus of Panama to Hudson bay?" Even Cuba was thought of by some as drawn inevitably by geographic laws toward union with the United States. Upon this idea two men as dissimilar as Thomas H. Benton and John Quincy Adams could agree. The island, thought Benton, was "the geographical appurtenance of the valley of the Mississippi and eventually to become its political appurtenance." Adams, as Secretary of State, likened Cuba to an apple which, when detached from the parent tree, would be drawn by a law of political gravitation to the United States.

What were the "natural boundaries" of the young republic? One mode of determining them was defined by Jefferson. Writing to Madison in 1809 of the hope of acquiring Cuba, he said: "Cuba can be defended by us without a navy, and this develops the principle which ought to limit our views. Nothing should ever be accepted which would require a navy to defend it." Northwardly, Jefferson visioned Canada as eventually to be drawn under the American flag; southwardly, Florida, Cuba, and probably Texas. On the west he apparently thought of the Rocky Mountains as forming the natural boundary. The West Coast would be peopled "with free and independent

Americans, unconnected with us but by the ties of blood and interest, and employing like us the rights of self-government." Sheer distance seemed an insuperable barrier to the incorporation of the Oregon country in the American Union. A representative from Oregon, it was asserted in 1825, if he visited his constituency once a year, would have but two weeks annually to spend in Washington; the remainder of the year would be spent in the journey to and fro. Even Senator Benton, who predicted that the future route to Asia would follow the Missouri and Columbia rivers, and who in 1825 argued in favor of military occupation of Oregon by the United States, believed that in settling that territory Americans would be planting the seed of a new republic. The natural western limit of the United States was "the ridge of the Rocky Mountains. . . . Along the back of this ridge, the Western limit of this republic should be drawn, and the statue of the fabled god, Terminus, should be raised upon its highest peak, never to be thrown down."

Such restricted ideas of the nation's natural boundaries were not to survive for many years. Indeed, some three years before Benton made this speech, the conservative weekly, *Niles' Register*, made an interesting prophecy. News had been received of the successful arrival at Santa Fe of one of the first parties of traders from Missouri. Commenting on this exploit, the *Register* predicted that crossing the Rockies would soon be as familiar to the western people as was the voyage to China to the easterners. "It was very possible that the citizens of St. Louis, on the *Mississippi*, may eat fresh salmon from the waters of the *Columbia!*—for distance seems as if annihilated by science and the spirit of adventure." On July 4, 1828, the people of Baltimore, amid elaborate ceremony, watched Charles Carroll, of Carrollton, lay the cornerstone that marked the beginning of the Baltimore and Ohio Railroad. In his address from the president and directors of the company, Mr. John B. Morris assumed the rôle of prophet. "We are," he said, "about affording facilities of intercourse between the east and the west, which will bind the one more closely to the other, beyond the power of an increased population or sectional difficulties to disunite. We are in fact commencing a new era in our history."

It was inevitable that the coming of the railroad and, later, of the telegraph should result in an expanding conception of the nation's natural boundaries. Daniel Webster could still maintain in 1845 that there would arise an independent "Pacific republic" on the west coast, but for many others the "throne of Terminus" had moved on from the Rockies to the shores of the Pacific. The *Democratic Review*, leading organ of the expansionists of the Mexican War era, predicted in 1845 that a railroad to the Pacific would soon be a reality, and that "the day cannot be far distant which shall witness the conveyance of the representatives from Oregon and California to Washington within less time than a few years ago was devoted to a similar journey by those from Ohio." The telegraph, furthermore, would soon enable Pacific coast newspapers "to set up in type the first half of the President's Inaugural, before the echoes of the latter half shall have died away beneath the lofty porch of the Capitol, as spoken from his lips." In the debate on the Oregon question in the House of Representatives in January, 1846, the significance of the Pacific as a natural boundary was repeatedly stressed. From the Atlantic to the Pacific, said Bowlin of Missouri, "we were by nature, ay, we were stamped by the hand of God himself, as one nation of men." Similarly, in the debate of 1844 and 1845 over the annexation of Texas, the Rio Grande with the neighboring strips of desert country had been portrayed as the divinely fixed natural boundary of the United States on the southwest.

If a divine hand had shaped the outlines of the North American continent with a view to its attaining political unity, the divine mind was thought to be by no means indifferent to the type of political organism which should dominate it. The American god of the early nineteenth century was the God of Democracy, and his followers had no doubt that he had reserved the continent for a democratic nation. Jefferson may not have regarded this consummation as a divinely appointed destiny, but he certainly contemplated as probable and desirable the spread of democratic institutions throughout the continent. The true flowering of this idea, however, belongs properly to the Jacksonian era, and its most enthusiastic exponent was the *Democratic Review*, a monthly magazine founded and for many years edited by Mr. John L. O'Sullivan. This exuberant Irish-American, whose faith in the institutions of his adopted country was irrepressible, not only coined the phrase "manifest destiny" but for years expounded in the pages of the *Review* the idea which it embodied.

The *Democratic Review* was founded in 1837. In the issue for November, 1839, appeared an article, presumably by O'Sullivan, entitled

"The Great Nation of Futurity." This rôle was to be America's, it was argued,

> because the principle upon which a nation is organized fixes its destiny, and that of equality is perfect, is universal. . . . Besides, the truthful annals of any nation furnish abundant evidence, that its happiness, its greatness, its duration, were always proportionate to the democratic equality in its system of government. . . . We point to the everlasting truth on the first page of our national declaration, and we proclaim to the millions of other lands, that "the gates of hell"—the powers of aristocracy and monarchy—"shall not prevail against it."

Thus happily founded upon the perfect principle of equality, the United States was destined to a unique success. Her shining example should "smite unto death the tyranny of kings, hierarchs, and oligarchs." What all this portended for the future boundaries of the United States the writer did not state except in poetic language. "Its floor shall be a hemisphere," he wrote, "its roof the firmament of the star-studded heavens, and its congregation an Union of many Republics, comprising hundreds of happy millions, . . . governed by God's natural and moral law of equality. . . ." Within a few years, however, the *Democratic Review* became sufficiently concrete in its ideas of the extent of the democratizing mission of the United States. Texas, Oregon, California, Canada, and much or all of Mexico, were to receive the blessings of American principles. The American continent had been reserved by Providence for the dawn of a new era, when men should be ready to throw off the antique systems of Europe and live in the light of equality and reason. The time was now at hand, and no American should shrink from the task of spreading the principles of liberty over all the continent. Cuba, too, had been left by Providence in the hands of a weak power until the United States was ready for it. Now it, like the rest, was "about to be annexed to the model republic."

The ideas so fervently preached in the *Democratic Review* were echoed in Congress and elsewhere. With reference to the Oregon controversy, James Buchanan asserted in 1844 that Providence had given to the American people the mission of "extending the blessings of Christianity and of civil and religious liberty over the whole North American continent." Breese of Illinois declared that "the impartial and the just" would see in the occupation of Oregon "a desire only to extend more widely the area of human freedom, . . . as an extension, sir, of that grand theatre, on which God, in his providence, and in his own appointed time, intends to work out that high destiny he has assigned for the whole human race." California was not forgotten. A letter from an American in that Mexican state, published in the *Baltimore Patriot*, commented on the way in which "our people, like a sure heavy and sullen tide, are overflowing the country"; and the writer declared that, while not himself an advocate of territorial aggression, he thought he could "foresee in the inevitable destiny of this territory, one of the most efficient fortresses from which new and liberal are to combat old and despotic institutions." Kaufman of Texas was sure the day was near "when not one atom of kingly power will disgrace the North American continent." Apologists for the war with Mexico were apt at urging its providential character and beneficent results. B. F. Porter, of Alabama, in an article on "The Mission of America," intimated that the war was a divine instrument for spreading American institutions and ideals to the Pacific; and Robert J. Walker, Secretary of the Treasury, inserted in his report for December, 1847, a paragraph gratefully acknowledging the aid of a "higher than any earthly power" which had guided American expansion in the past and which "still guards and directs our destiny, impels us onward, and has selected our great and happy country as a model and ultimate centre of attraction for all the nations of the world."

Neither natural boundaries nor divinely favored institutions were in themselves sufficient to insure the peopling of the continent by the favored race. The third essential factor was seen in what more than one Congressman termed "the American multiplication table." "Go to the West," said Kennedy of Indiana in 1846, "and see a young man with his mate of eighteen; after the lapse of thirty years, visit him again and instead of two, you will find twenty-two. This is what I call the American multiplication table." Apparently Jefferson had in mind this same fecundity of the Anglo-Saxon race in America when he predicted in 1786 that "our confederacy must be viewed as the nest from which all America, North & South, is to be peopled," and when in 1803 he expressed full confidence in the growth of such an American population on the Mississippi "as will be able to do their own business" in securing control of New Orleans. On the same principle, Barbour of Virginia foretold in 1825 the peopling of the Oregon country by Americans.

It was partly, too, upon the basis of this unexampled growth in numbers that the editor of the *Democratic Review* founded his doctrine of "manifest destiny." It was in an unsigned article in the number for July–August, 1845, that the phrase first appeared. The writer charged foreign nations with attempting to impede the annexation of Texas, with the object of "checking the fulfilment of our manifest destiny to overspread the continent allotted by Providence for the free development of our yearly multiplying millions." Texas, he said, had been

> absorbed into the Union in the inevitable fulfilment of the general law which is rolling our population westward; the connexion of which with that ratio of growth in population which is destined within a hundred years to swell our numbers to the enormous population of *two hundred and fifty millions* (if not more), is too evident to leave us in doubt of the manifest design of Providence in regard to the occupation of this continent.

When war with Mexico came, and the more rabid expansionists were seeking excuses for annexing large portions of Mexican territory, a different side of the idea of racial superiority was advanced. The Mexicans, it seemed, had a destiny too—how different from that of their northern neighbors! "The Mexican race," said the *Democratic Review*, "now see, in the fate of the aborigines of the north, their own inevitable destiny. They must amalgamate and be lost, in the superior vigor of the Anglo-Saxon race, or they must utterly perish." The *New York Evening Post* indorsed the idea, sanctifying it in the name of Providence. "Providence has so ordained it; and it is folly not to recognize the fact. The Mexicans are *aboriginal Indians*, and they must share the destiny of their race."

This pre-Darwinian version of the "survival of the fittest" was branded by the aged Albert Gallatin, an opponent of the war, as "a most extraordinary assertion." That it persisted, that it constituted, in the 1850's, an integral part of the concept of manifest destiny is clear from the remarks of both friends and foes. John L. O'Sullivan was serving in 1855 as United States minister to Portugal. He reported to

Secretary Marcy a conversation with some French imperialists in which he had said:

> I should be as glad to see our common race and blood overspread all Africa under the French flag and all India under the British, as they ought to be to see it overspread all the Western hemisphere under ours; and that probably enough that was the plan of Providence; to which we in America were accustomed to give the name of "manifest destiny."

On the other hand, George Fitzhugh of Virginia, who believed in institutions (such as slavery) for the protection of weaker races, charged the members of the "Young American" party in Congress with boasting "that the Anglo-Saxon race is manifestly destined to eat out all the other races, as the wiregrass destroys and takes the place of other grasses," and with inviting admiration for "this war of nature" —admiration which Fitzhugh, for one, refused to concede.

Thus manifest destiny, which must be thought of as embracing all the ideas hitherto considered—geographical determinism, the superiority of democratic institutions, the superior fecundity, stamina, and ability of the white race—became a justification for almost any addition of territory which the United States had the will and the power to obtain.

Such ideas were not, as has been rather generally assumed, peculiarly southern. In their extreme form, at least, both the ideas and the imperialistic program which they were used to justify were repudiated by southern Whig leaders, and even by John C. Calhoun himself. The southerner most closely associated with the program, Robert J. Walker, was of northern birth, was by no means an unwavering supporter of slavery, and was presently to sever entirely his connections with the South. The inventor of the phrase "manifest destiny" and one of the most persevering advocates of expansion was, as has been said, John L. O'Sullivan, who described himself in a letter to Calhoun as a "New York Free Soiler"; and he had the friendship and sympathy of prominent northern Democrats like Buchanan, Marcy, and Pierce. Indeed, if the manifest destiny of the 1840's and 1850's must be classified, it should be described as Democratic rather than sectional. Yet, even this generalization will not bear too close scrutiny, for William H. Seward, an antislavery Whig and Republican, was scarcely less intrigued by the idea than O'Sullivan himself. As early as 1846 he was predicting that the population of the United States was "destined to roll its resistless waves to the icy barriers of the North, and to encounter oriental civilization on the shores of the Pacific"; and in a speech at St. Paul, Minnesota, in 1860, he asserted with assurance that Russian, Canadian, and Latin on the American continents were but laying the foundations for future states of the American republic, whose ultimate capital would be the City of Mexico.

Seward, in fact, supplies the chief link between the manifest destiny of the pre-Civil War years and the expansionist schemes of the decade following the war. As Secretary of State he had an opportunity to try his hand at a program of expansion; and though of all his plans the purchase of Alaska alone was carried through, the discussions of that and of other proposed acquisitions—the Danish West Indies, the Dominican Republic, the Hawaiian Islands, and Canada—demonstrated the continuity of ideas from 1850 to 1870. Professor T. C. Smith, who made an analysis of the expansionist arguments used in this period, found annexations urged on four principal grounds: economic value, strategic value to the navy, extension of republican institutions, and geographic determinism. Only the second of these—the naval base argument—was at all new. It owed its vogue at the time to the navy's difficulties during the war. The first was always to be met with, and the third and fourth were carry-overs from the days of manifest destiny.

The collapse of the expansionist program of Seward and Grant was followed by a general loss of interest in such enterprises, which did not recover their one-time popularity until the era of the Spanish-American War. In the meantime, however, new arguments were taking shape which would eventually impinge on the popular consciousness and raise almost as keen an interest in expansion as that which had elected Polk in 1844. But while manifest destiny was a product indigenous to the United States, some of the new doctrines owed their origin to European trends of thought.

In 1859 Charles Darwin published his *Origin of Species*, setting forth the hypothesis that the evolution of the higher forms of life had come about through the preservation and perpetuation of chance variations by the "survival of the fittest" in the never ending struggle for existence. The authoritativeness of this work, and the stir which it made in the scientific world, gave a scientific sanction to the idea that perpetual struggle in the political and social world would lead up-ward along the evolutionary path. Many were the applications that might be made of such a principle—especially by nations and peoples considering themselves highly "fit." A nation with a faith in its politi-cal, moral, or racial superiority might take pleasure in the thought that in crushing its inferior neighbors it was at once obeying the law of destiny and contributing to the perfection of the species.

What did Darwinism signify for the future of the United States? One of the first to attempt an answer to that riddle was the historian, John Fiske, who spoke with double authority as a student of Amer-ican institutions and a follower and popularizer of Darwin. Fiske's conclusion was sufficiently gratifying. Anglo-Saxons in the United States had evolved the "fittest" of all political principles—federalism—upon which all the world would at some future day be organized. Anglo-Saxons, moreover, excelled not only in institutions but in growth of numbers and economic power. So evident was the superior "fitness" of this race that its expansion was certain to go on "until every land on the earth's surface that is not already the seat of an old civilization shall become English in its language, in its religion, in its political habits and traditions, and to a predominant extent in the blood of its people." "The day is at hand," said Fiske, "when four-fifths of the human race will trace its pedigree to English forefathers, as four-fifths of the white people of the United States trace their pedigree today." This was surely encouraging doctrine to Americans or British who wanted an excuse to go a-conquering.

Conclusions very similar to Fiske's were reached by Josiah Strong, a Congregational clergyman, who in 1885 published what became a popular and widely read book entitled *Our Country: Its Possible Future and Its Present Crisis.* The Anglo-Saxon, thought Strong, as the chief representative of the two most valuable civilizing forces—civil liberty and "a pure *spiritual* Christianity"—was being divinely schooled for "*the final competition of races. . . .*" "If I read not amiss," he said, "this powerful race will move down upon Mexico, down upon Central and South America, out upon the islands of the sea, over upon Africa and beyond. And can any one doubt that the result of this competition of races will be the 'survival of the fittest'?" The extinction of inferior races before the conquering Anglo-Saxon might appear sad to some; but Strong knew of nothing likely to prevent it, and he accepted it as part of the divine plan. His doctrine was a curious blending of religious and scientific dogma.

If Fiske and Strong could show that expansion was a matter of destiny, another scholar of the day preached it as a duty. In his *Political Science and Comparative Constitutional Law*, published in 1890, John W. Burgess, of Columbia University, surveyed the political careers of the principal civilized races and concluded that, of them all, only the Teutonic group had talent of the highest order. Greek and Roman, Slav and Celt, had exhibited their various abilities. Some had excelled in building city-states; others, in planning world-empires. Only Teutons had learned the secret of the national state, the form fittest to survive. The Teutonic nations—German and Anglo-Saxon— were "the political nations *par excellence*," and this pre-eminence gave them the right "in the economy of the world to assume the leadership in the establishment and administration of states." Especially were they called "to carry the political civilization of the modern world into those parts of the world inhabited by unpolitical and barbaric races; i.e. they must have a colonial policy." There was "no human right to the status of barbarism." If barbaric peoples resisted the civilizing efforts of the political nations, the latter might rightly reduce them to subjection or clear their territory of their presence. If a population were not barbaric but merely incompetent politically, then too the Teutonic nations might "righteously assume sovereignty over, and undertake to create state order for, such a politically incompetent population."

There is in these pages of Burgess such a complete justification not only for British and German imperialism but also for the course of acquiring colonies and protectorates upon which the United States was to embark in 1898 that one learns with surprise from his rather naïve autobiography that Burgess was profoundly shocked by the war with Spain and felt that the adoption of an imperialistic career was a colossal blunder. One would have supposed that he would have rejoiced that his country was assuming its share of world responsibility as one of the Teutonic nations.

To Fiske and Strong, expansion was destiny; to Burgess, it was duty, though he apparently excused his own country from any share in its performance. To Alfred Thayer Mahan, the historian and prophet who frankly assumed the rôle of propagandist, it was both duty and opportunity. Mahan's *Influence of Sea Power upon History,* the result of a series of lectures at the Naval War College at Newport, Rhode Island, was published in 1890. Other books on naval history followed, but it is likely that Mahan reached a wider American public through the many magazine articles which he published at frequent intervals during the ensuing decade. History, as Mahan wrote it, was no mere academic exercise. Searching the past for lessons applicable to the here and now, he found them in full measure. Rather, he found *one,* which he never tired of driving home: Sea power was essential to national greatness. Sea power embraced commerce, merchant marine, navy, naval bases whence commerce might be protected, and colonies where it might find its farther terminals. One nation, Great Britain, had learned this lesson by heart and practiced it faithfully, with results that Mahan thought admirable. One other nation, he hoped, might walk in her footsteps.

Certain specific needs, beside the obvious one of a stronger navy and better coast defenses, Mahan urged upon his countrymen. If an Isthmian canal were to be built, the United States ought to build and control it, or failing this, to control completely the approaches to it. This involved a willingness to accept islands in the Caribbean whenever they could be had by righteous means; sheer acts of conquest Mahan repudiated. It involved also a willingness to accept the Hawaiian Islands, partly as an outpost to the Pacific end of the canal, partly for another reason which weighed heavily with Mahan. The Pacific, he believed, was to be the theater of a vast conflict between Occident and Orient, with the United States holding the van of the Western forces. His deep religious sense assured him that the Deity was preparing the Christian powers for that coming cataclysm, but he was equally sure that mere human agents must keep their powder dry. The United States must be ready, with a navy, a canal, and as many island outposts as she could righteously acquire, for her share in the great struggle between civilizations and religions. Even the practical-minded naval officer must have a cosmic justification for the policy of national imperialism which he advocated.

It was such ideas as these of Fiske, Strong, Burgess, and Mahan which created a public opinion receptive to expansion overseas in 1898. Theodore Roosevelt and Henry Cabot Lodge, whose influence upon the events of that year was large indeed, were under the spell of

Mahan's writings. Roosevelt had been a pupil of Burgess while studying law at Columbia. In the debate over imperialism which ensued,
the argument from Anglo-Saxon or Teutonic superiority and the divinely appointed mission of the race was probably as influential as the
more practical strategic and economic arguments. Kipling's contribution, "The White Man's Burden," which appeared in 1898, fitted in
well with the American temper. In the United States Senate, young
Albert J. Beveridge, using language that might almost have been taken
bodily from Burgess' treatise, declared that God "has made us [Anglo-
Saxons and Teutons] the master organizers of the world to establish
system where chaos reigns. . . . He has made us adepts in government that we may administer government among savage and senile
peoples." William Allen White, in the *Emporia Gazette*, proclaimed:
"Only Anglo-Saxons can govern themselves. . . . It is the Anglo-
Saxon's manifest destiny to go forth as a world conqueror. He will
take possession of the islands of the sea. . . . This is what fate holds
for the chosen people." Senator O. H. Platt wrote President McKinley
that in Connecticut "those who believe in Providence, see, or think
they see, that God has placed upon this Government the solemn duty
of providing for the people of these islands [the Philippines] a government based upon the principle of liberty no matter how many
difficulties the problem may present." A missionary from China was
quoted as saying: "You will find that all American missionaries are in
favor of expansion."

Even those who stressed the economic value of new possessions
could not refrain from claiming the special interest of Providence.
That the war with Spain and the victory in the Philippines should have
come just as the European powers were attempting to partition China
and monopolize its markets, seemed to the *American Banker* of New
York "a coincidence which has a providential air." Familiar to all
students of the period is McKinley's story of how he prayed for divine
guidance as to the disposition of the Philippines, and of how "one
night it came to me this way—I don't know how it was but it came:
. . . that we could not turn them over to France or Germany—our
commercial rivals in the Orient—that would be bad business and discreditable." Reasons of a more ideal character were vouchsafed to William McKinley on the same occasion, but McKinley's God did not
hesitate to converse with him in terms that might better have befitted

Mark Hanna. Perhaps McKinley did not misunderstand. Josiah Strong was a clergyman and hence in a better position than McKinley to interpret the wishes of the Deity; yet he found in Providence a concern for American business similar to that which McKinley detected. Strong, too, had in mind the Philippines and especially their relation to China and to the maintenance of the Open Door in the markets of that developing empire.

> And when we remember [he wrote] that our new necessities [markets for our manufactures] are precisely complementary to China's new needs, it is not difficult to see a providential meaning in the fact that, with no design of our own, we have become an Asiatic power, close to the Yellow Sea, and we find it easy to believe that

> "There's a divinity that shapes our ends,
> Rough-hew them how we will."

Expansionists of different periods had invoked a God of Nature, a God of Democracy, a God of Evolution. It seems appropriate enough that those who inaugurated the last phase of territorial expansion, at the close of the nineteenth century, should have proclaimed their faith in a God of Business.

The Cult of True Womanhood: 1820–1860

BARBARA WELTER

• Woman's role has been subject to controversy since the time she was fashioned from Adam's rib. In America, Thomas Paine noted as early as 1775 that women were "constrained in their desires, in the disposal of their goods, robbed of freedom and will by the laws, the slaves of opinions." In the nineteenth century, the American feminist movement was activated with the movement to free slaves. Such women as Lucy Stone, Margaret Fuller, and Elizabeth Cady Stanton worked for abolition and temperance, but directed their main energies to female rights in property ownership, education, and job opportunity. In 1848 the first Women's Rights Convention met in Seneca Falls, New York, and accepted as a self-evident truth "that all men and women are created equal." This proclamation had little effect on the national temper, however, and a half-century later women still remained second-class citizens in the United States.

In the first part of the twentieth century, the feminist movement concentrated its efforts on universal suffrage, and though the leaders were castigated as man-eaters and unnatural monsters for attempting to destroy the "God-given subservience of woman," they achieved the right to vote with the Nineteenth Amendment which went into effect in 1920.

Feminism waned as a vital force in American life after 920, but encouraged by the ideals of the black revolution in the 1960's, the movement for women's rights revived. Seeking a revolution in attitudes and behavior, militant women burned their bras, picketed the Miss America pageant, and demonstrated against discrimination in hiring and salary procedures. Feminists were especially critical of popular women's magazines for projecting "a destructive image of women."

From *American Quarterly*, Vol. XVIII, no. 2, part 1, pp. 151–174 (1966). Copyright © 1966, Trustees of the University of Pennsylvania. Reprinted by permission of the journal, the author, and University of Pennsylvania, publisher.

In The Feminine Mystique, Betty Friedan castigated the fe-
male press for characterizing the "happy housewife" as "young
and frivolous, almost childlike, fluffy and feminine, passive,
gaily content in a world of bedroom and kitchen, sex, babies
and home."

The indictment was not a new one. In the following arti-
cle, Barbara Welter holds early nineteenth-century periodi-
cals and other pieces of popular literature accountable for
nurturing the cult of true womanhood. While the choice
today is usually between home and career, the choice a cen-
tury and more ago was presumably either a life of de-
votion, purity, and virtue or an existence characterized by
depravity and the desires of the flesh. And these images were
clearly defined by the popular press of the nineteenth cen-
tury. Are periodicals themselves powerful enough to shape
woman's role in society or are other factors of equal or greater
importance? Has the image of women changed in the last
century to a substantial degree?

The nineteenth-century American man was a busy builder of bridges
and railroads, at work long hours in a materialistic society. The religious values of his forebears were neglected in practice if not in
intent, and he occasionally felt some guilt that he had turned this new
land, this temple of the chosen people, into one vast countinghouse.
But he could salve his conscience by reflecting that he had left behind
a hostage, not only to fortune, but to all the values which he held so
dear and treated so lightly. Woman, in the cult of True Womanhood
presented by the women's magazines, gift annuals and religious literature of the nineteenth century, was the hostage in the home. In a
society where the values changed frequently, where fortunes rose and
fell with frightening rapidity, where social and economic mobility
provided instability as well as hope, one thing at least remained the
same—a true woman was a true woman, wherever she was found. If
anyone, male or female, dared to tamper with the complex of vir-

tues which made up True Womanhood, he was damned immediately as an enemy of God, of civilization and of the Republic. It was a fearful obligation, a solemn responsibility, which the nineteenth-century American woman had—to uphold the pillars of the temple with her frail white hand.

The attributes of True Womanhood, by which a woman judged herself and was judged by her husband, her neighbors and society could be divided into four cardinal virtues—piety, purity, submissiveness and domesticity. Put them all together and they spelled mother, daughter, sister, wife—woman. Without them, no matter whether there was fame, achievement or wealth, all was ashes. With them she was promised happiness and power.

Religion or piety was the core of woman's virtue, the source of her strength. Young men looking for a mate were cautioned to search first for piety, for if that were there, all else would follow. Religion belonged to woman by divine right, a gift of God and nature. This "peculiar susceptibility" to religion was given her for a reason: "the vestal flame of piety, lighted up by Heaven in the breast of woman" would throw its beams into the naughty world of men. So far would its candle power reach that the "Universe might be Enlightened, Improved, and Harmonized by woman!!" She would be another, better Eve, working in cooperation with the Redeemer, bringing the world back "from its revolt and sin." The world would be reclaimed for God through her suffering, for "God increased the cares and sorrows of woman, that she might be sooner constrained to accept the terms of salvation." A popular poem by Mrs. Frances Osgood, "The Triumph of the Spiritual Over the Sensual" expressed just this sentiment, woman's purifying passionless love bringing an erring man back to Christ.

Dr. Charles Meigs, explaining to a graduating class of medical students why women were naturally religious, said that "hers is a pious mind. Her confiding nature leads her more readily than men to accept the proffered grace of the Gospel." Caleb Atwater, Esq., writing in *The Ladies' Repository*, saw the hand of the Lord in female piety: "Religion is exactly what a woman needs, for it gives her that dignity that best suits her dependence." And Mrs. John Sandford, who had no very high opinion of her sex, agreed thoroughly: "Religion is just what woman needs. Without it she is ever restless or unhappy. . . ." Mrs. Sandford and the others did not speak only of that restlessness of the human heart, which St. Augustine notes, that can only find its peace in God. They spoke rather of religion as a kind of tranquilizer for the many undefined longings which swept even the most pious young girl, and about which it was better to pray than to think.

One reason religion was valued was that it did not take a woman away from her "proper sphere," her home. Unlike participation in other societies or movements, church work would not make her less domestic or submissive, less a True Woman. In religious vineyards, said the *Young Ladies' Literary and Missionary Report*, "you may labor without the apprehension of detracting from the charms of feminine delicacy." Mrs. S. L. Dagg, writing from her chapter of the Society in Tuscaloosa, Alabama, was equally reassuring: "As no sensible woman will suffer her intellectual pursuits to clash with her domestic duties" she should concentrate on religious work "which promotes these very duties."

The women's seminaries aimed at aiding women to be religious, as well as accomplished. Mt. Holyoke's catalogue promised to make female education "a handmaid to the Gospel and an efficient auxiliary in the great task of renovating the world." The Young Ladies' Seminary at Bordentown, New Jersey, declared its most important function to be "the forming of a sound and virtuous character." In Keene, New Hampshire, the Seminary tried to instill a "consistent and useful character" in its students, to enable them in this life to be "a good friend, wife and mother" but more important, to qualify them for "the enjoyment of Celestial Happiness in the life to come." And Joseph M' D. Mathews, Principal of Oakland Female Seminary in Hillsborough, Ohio, believed that "female education should be preeminently religious."

If religion was so vital to a woman, irreligion was almost too awful to contemplate. Women were warned not to let their literary or intellectual pursuits take them away from God. Sarah Josepha Hale spoke darkly of those who, like Margaret Fuller, threw away the "One True Book" for others, open to error. Mrs. Hale used the unfortunate Miss Fuller as fateful proof that "the greater the intellectual force, the greater and more fatal the errors into which women fall who wander from the Rock of Salvation, Christ the Saviour. . . ."

One gentleman, writing on "Female Irreligion" reminded his readers that "Man may make himself a brute, and does so very often, but can woman brutify herself to his level—the lowest level of human nature—without exerting special wonder?" Fanny Wright, because she was godless, "was no woman, mother though she be." A few years ago, he recalls, such women would have been whipped. In any case, "woman never looks lovelier than in her reverence for religion" and, conversely, "female irreligion is the most revolting feature in human character."

Purity was as essential as piety to a young woman, its absence as unnatural and unfeminine. Without it she was, in fact, no woman at all, but a member of some lower order. A "fallen woman" was a "fallen angel," unworthy of the celestial company of her sex. To contemplate the loss of purity brought tears; to be guilty of such a crime, in the women's magazines at least, brought madness or death. Even the language of the flowers had bitter words for it: a dried white rose symbolized "Death Preferable to Loss of Innocence." The marriage night was the single great event of a woman's life, when she bestowed her greatest treasure upon her husband, and from that time on was completely dependent upon him, an empty vessel, without legal or emotional existence of her own.

Therefore all True Women were urged, in the strongest possible terms, to maintain their virtue, although men, being by nature more sensual than they, would try to assault it. Thomas Branagan admitted in *The Excellency of the Female Character Vindicated* that his sex would sin and sin again, they could not help it, but woman, stronger and purer, must not give in and let man "take liberties incompatible with her delicacy." "If you do," Branagan addressed his gentle reader, "You will be left in silent sadness to bewail your credulity, imbecility, duplicity, and premature prostitution."

Mrs. Eliza Farrar, in *The Young Lady's Friend*, gave practical logistics to avoid trouble: "Sit not with another in a place that is too narrow; read not out of the same book; let not your eagerness to see anything induce you to place your head close to another person's."

If such good advice was ignored the consequences were terrible and inexorable. In *Girlhood and Womanhood: Or Sketches of My Schoolmates*, by Mrs. A. J. Graves (a kind of mid-nineteenth-century *The Group*), the bad ends of a boarding school class of girls are scrupulously recorded. The worst end of all is reserved for "Amelia Dorrington: The Lost One." Amelia died in the almshouse "the wretched victim of depravity and intemperance" and all because her mother had let her be "high-spirited not prudent." These girlish high spirits had been misinterpreted by a young man, with disastrous results. Amelia's "thoughtless levity" was "followed by a total loss of virtuous principle" and Mrs. Graves editorializes that "the coldest reserve is more admirable in a woman a man wishes to make his wife, than the least approach to undue familiarity."

A popular and often-reprinted story by Fanny Forester told the sad tale of "Lucy Dutton." Lucy "with the seal of innocence upon her heart, and a rose-leaf on her cheek" came out of her vine-covered cottage and ran into a city slicker. "And Lucy was beautiful and trusting, and thoughtless: and he was gay, selfish and profligate. Needs the story to be told? . . . Nay, censor, Lucy was a child—consider how young, how very untaught—oh! her innocence was no match for the sophistry of a gay, city youth! Spring came and shame was stamped upon the cottage at the foot of the hill." The baby died; Lucy went mad at the funeral and finally died herself. "Poor, poor Lucy Dutton! The grave is a blessed couch and pillow to the wretched. Rest thee there, poor Lucy!" The frequency with which derangement follows loss of virtue suggests the exquisite sensibility of woman, and the possibility that, in the women's magazines at least, her intellect was geared to her hymen, not her brain.

If, however, a woman managed to withstand man's assaults on her virtue, she demonstrated her superiority and her power over him. Eliza Farnham, trying to prove this female superiority, concluded smugly that "the purity of women is the everlasting barrier against which the tides of man's sensual nature surge."

A story in The Lady's Amaranth illustrates this dominance. It is set, improbably, in Sicily, where two lovers, Bianca and Tebaldo, have been separated because her family insisted she marry a rich old man. By some strange circumstance the two are in a shipwreck and cast on a desert island, the only survivors. Even here, however, the rigid standards of True Womanhood prevail. Tebaldo unfortunately forgets himself slightly, so that Bianca must warn him: "We may not indeed gratify our fondness by caresses, but it is still something to bestow our kindest language, and looks and prayers, and all lawful and honest attentions on each other." Something, perhaps, but not enough, and Bianca must further remonstrate: "It is true that another man is my husband, but you are my guardian angel." When even that does not work she says in a voice of sweet reason, passive and proper to the end, that she wishes he wouldn't but "still, if you insist, I will become what you wish; but I beseech you to consider, ere that decision, that debasement which I must suffer in your esteem." This appeal to his own double standards holds the beast in him at bay. They are rescued, discover that the old husband is dead, and after "mourning a decent season" Bianca finally gives in, legally.

Men could be counted on to be grateful when women thus saved them from themselves. William Alcott, guiding young men in their relations with the opposite sex, told them that "Nothing is better calculated to preserve a young man from contamination of low pleasures and pursuits than frequent intercourse with the more refined and virtuous of the other sex." And he added, one assumes in equal innocence, that youths should "observe and learn to admire, that purity and ignorance of evil which is the characteristic of well-educated young ladies, and which, when we are near them, raises us above those sordid and sensual considerations which hold such sway over men in their intercourse with each other."

The Rev. Jonathan F. Stearns was also impressed by female chastity in the face of male passion, and warned woman never to compromise the source of her power: "Let her lay aside delicacy, and her influence over our sex is gone."

Women themselves accepted, with pride but suitable modesty, this priceless virtue. *The Ladies' Wreath*, in "Woman the Creature of God and the Manufacturer of Society" saw purity as her greatest gift and chief means of discharging her duty to save the world: "Purity is the highest beauty—the true pole-star which is to guide humanity aright in its long, varied, and perilous voyage."

Sometimes, however, a woman did not see the dangers to her treasure. In that case, they must be pointed out to her, usually by a male. In the nineteenth century any form of social change was tantamount to an attack on woman's virtue, if only it was correctly understood. For example, dress reform seemed innocuous enough and the bloomers worn by the lady of that name and her followers were certainly modest attire. Such was the reasoning only of the ignorant. In another issue of *The Ladies' Wreath* a young lady is represented in dialogue with her "Professor." The girl expresses admiration for the bloomer costume—it gives freedom of motion, is healthful and attractive. The "Professor" sets her straight. Trousers, he explains, are "only one of the many manifestations of that wild spirit of socialism and agrarian radicalism which is at present so rife in our land." The young lady recants immediately: "If this dress has any connexion with Fourierism or Socialism, or fanaticism in any shape whatever, I have no disposition to wear it at all . . . no true woman would so far compromise her delicacy as to espouse, however unwittingly, such a cause."

America could boast that her daughters were particularly innocent. In a poem on "The American Girl" the author wrote proudly:

> Her eye of light is the diamond bright,
> Her innocence the pearl,
> And these are ever the bridal gems
> That are worn by the American girl.

Lydia Maria Child, giving advice to mothers, aimed at preserving that spirit of innocence. She regretted that "want of confidence between mothers and daughters on delicate subjects" and suggested a woman tell her daughter a few facts when she reached the age of twelve to "set her mind at rest." Then Mrs. Child confidently hoped that a young lady's "instinctive modesty" would "prevent her from dwelling on the information until she was called upon to use it." In the same vein, a book of advice to the newly-married was titled *Whisper to a Bride*. As far as intimate information was concerned, there was no need to whisper, since the book contained none at all.

A masculine summary of this virtue was expressed in a poem "Female Charms":

> I would have her as pure as the snow on the mount—
>   As true as the smile that to infamy's given—
> As pure as the wave of the crystalline fount,
>   Yet as warm in the heart as the sunlight of heaven.
> With a mind cultivated, not boastingly wise,
>   I could gaze on such beauty, with exquisite bliss;
> With her heart on her lips and her soul in her eyes—
>   What more could I wish in dear woman than this.

Man might, in fact, ask no more than this in woman, but she was beginning to ask more of herself, and in the asking was threatening the third powerful and necessary virtue, submission. Purity, considered as a moral imperative, set up a dilemma which was hard to resolve. Woman must preserve her virtue until marriage and marriage was necessary for her happiness. Yet marriage was, literally, an end to innocence. She was told not to question this dilemma, but simply to accept it.

Submission was perhaps the most feminine virtue expected of women. Men were supposed to be religious, although they rarely had time for it, and supposed to be pure, although it came awfully hard to them, but men were the movers, the doers, the actors. Women were the passive, submissive responders. The order of dialogue was, of course, fixed in Heaven. Man was "woman's superior by God's appointment, if not in intellectual dowry, at least by official decree." Therefore, as Charles Elliott argued in *The Ladies' Repository*, she should submit to him "for the sake of good order at least." In *The Ladies Companion* a young wife was quoted approvingly as saying that she did not think woman should "feel and act for herself" because "When, next to God, her husband is not the tribunal to which her heart and intellect appeals—the golden bowl of affection is broken." Women were warned that if they tampered with this quality they tampered with the order of the Universe.

The Young Lady's Book summarized the necessity of the passive virtues in its readers' lives: "It is, however, certain, that in whatever situation of life a woman is placed from her cradle to her grave, a spirit of obedience and submission, pliability of temper, and humility of mind, are required from her."

Woman understood her position if she was the right kind of woman, a true woman. "She feels herself weak and timid. She needs a protector," declared George Burnap, in his lectures on *The Sphere and Duties of Woman*. "She is in a measure dependent. She asks for wisdom, constancy, firmness, perseverance, and she is willing to repay it all by the surrender of the full treasure of her affections. Woman despises in man every thing like herself except a tender heart. It is enough that she is effeminate and weak; she does not want another like herself." Or put even more strongly by Mrs. Sandford: "A really sensible woman feels her dependence. She does what she can, but she is conscious of inferiority, and therefore grateful for support."

Mrs. Sigourney, however, assured young ladies that although they were separate, they were equal. This difference of the sexes did not imply inferiority, for it was part of that same order of Nature established by Him "who bids the oak brave the fury of the tempest, and the alpine flower lean its cheek on the bosom of eternal snows." Dr. Meigs had a different analogy to make the same point, contrasting the anatomy of the Apollo of the Belvedere (illustrating the male principle) with the Venus de Medici (illustrating the female principle). "Woman," said the physician, with a kind of clinical gallantry, "has a head almost too small for intellect but just big enough for love."

This love itself was to be passive and responsive. "Love, in the heart of a woman," wrote Mrs. Farrar, "should partake largely of the nature of gratitude. She should love, because she is already loved by one deserving her regard."

Woman was to work in silence, unseen, like Wordsworth's Lucy. Yet, "working like nature, in secret" her love goes forth to the world "to regulate its pulsation, and send forth from its heart, in pure and temperate flow, the life-giving current." She was to work only for pure affection, without thought of money or ambition. A poem, "Woman and Fame," by Felicia Hemans, widely quoted in many of the gift books, concludes with a spirited renunciation of the gift of fame:

> Away! to me, a woman, bring
> Sweet flowers from affection's spring.

"True feminine genius," said Grace Greenwood (Sara Jane Clarke) "is ever timid, doubtful, and clingingly dependent; a perpetual childhood." And she advised literary ladies in an essay on "The Intellectual Woman"—"Don't trample on the flowers while longing for the stars." A wife who submerged her own talents to work for her husband was extolled as an example of a true woman. In *Women of Worth: A Book for Girls*, Mrs. Ann Flaxman, an artist of promise herself, was praised because she "devoted herself to sustain her husband's genius and aid him in his arduous career."

Caroline Gilman's advice to the bride aimed at establishing this proper order from the beginning of marriage: "Oh, young and lovely bride, watch well the first moments when your will conflicts with his to whom God and society have given the control. Reverence his *wishes* even when you do not his *opinions*."

Mrs. Gilman's perfect wife in *Recollections of a Southern Matron* realizes that "the three golden threads with which domestic happiness is woven" are "to repress a harsh answer, to confess a fault, and to stop (right or wrong) in the midst of self-defense, in gentle submission." Woman could do this, hard though it was, because in her heart she knew she was right and so could afford to be forgiving, even a trifle condescending. "Men are not unreasonable," averred Mrs. Gilman. "Their difficulties lie in not understanding the moral and physical nature of our sex. They often wound through ignorance, and are surprised at having offended." Wives were advised to do their best to reform men, but if they couldn't, to give up gracefully. "If any habit of his annoyed me, I spoke of it once or twice, calmly, then bore it quietly."

A wife should occupy herself "only with domestic affairs—wait till your husband confides to you those of a high importance—and do not give your advice until he asks for it," advised the *Lady's Token*. At all times she should behave in a manner becoming a woman, who had "no arms other than gentleness." Thus "if he is abusive, never retort." A *Young Lady's Guide to the Harmonious Development of a Christian Character* suggested that females should "become as little children" and "avoid a controversial spirit." *The Mother's Assistant and Young Lady's Friend* listed "Always Conciliate" as its first commandment in "Rules for Conjugal and Domestic Happiness." Small wonder that these same rules ended with the succinct maxim: "Do not expect too much."

As mother, as well as wife, woman was required to submit to fortune. In *Letters to Mothers* Mrs. Sigourney sighed: "To bear the evils and sorrows which may be appointed us, with a patient mind, should be the continual effort of our sex. . . . It seems, indeed, to be expected of us; since the passive and enduring virtues are more immediately within our province." Of these trials "the hardest was to bear the loss of children with submission" but the indomitable Mrs. Sigourney found strength to murmur to the bereaved mother: "The

Lord loveth a cheerful giver." *The Ladies' Parlor Companion* agreed thoroughly in "A Submissive Mother," in which a mother who had already buried two children and was nursing a dying baby saw her sole remaining child "probably scalded to death. Handing over the infant to die in the arms of a friend, she bowed in sweet submission to the double stroke." But the child "through the goodness of God survived, and the mother learned to say 'Thy will be done.'"

Woman then, in all her roles, accepted submission as her lot. It was a lot she had not chosen or deserved. As *Godey's* said, "the lesson of submission is forced upon woman." Without comment or criticism the writer affirms that "To suffer and to be silent under suffering seems the great command she has to obey." George Burnap referred to a woman's life as "a series of suppressed emotions." She was, as Emerson said, "more vulnerable, more infirm, more mortal than man." The death of a beautiful woman, cherished in fiction, represented woman as the innocent victim, suffering without sin, too pure and good for this world but too weak and passive to resist its evil forces. The best refuge for such a delicate creature was the warmth and safety of her home.

The true woman's place was unquestionably by her own fireside—as daughter, sister, but most of all as wife and mother. Therefore domesticity was among the virtues most prized by the women's magazines. "As society is constituted," wrote Mrs. S. E. Farley, on the "Domestic and Social Claims on Woman," "the true dignity and beauty of the female character seem to consist in a right understanding and faithful and cheerful performance of social and family duties." Sacred Scripture re-enforced social pressure: "St. Paul knew what was best for women when he advised them to be domestic," said Mrs. Sandford. "There is composure at home; there is something sedative in the duties which home involves. It affords security not only from the world, but from delusions and errors of every kind."

From her home woman performed her great task of bringing men back to God. *The Young Ladies' Class Book* was sure that "the domestic fireside is the great guardian of society against the excesses of human passions." *The Lady at Home* expressed its convictions in its very title and concluded that "even if we cannot reform the world in a moment, we can begin the work by reforming ourselves and our households—It is woman's mission. Let her not look away from her own little family circle for the means of producing moral and social reforms, but begin at home."

Home was supposed to be a cheerful place, so that brothers, husbands and sons would not go elsewhere in search of a good time. Woman was expected to dispense comfort and cheer. In writing the biography of Margaret Mercer (every inch a true woman) her biographer (male) notes: "She never forgot that it is the peculiar province of woman to minister to the comfort, and promote the happiness, first, of those most nearly allied to her, and then of those, who by the Province of God are placed in a state of dependence upon her." Many other essays in the women's journals showed woman as comforter: "Woman, Man's Best Friend," "Woman, the Greatest Social Benefit," "Woman, A Being to Come Home To," "The Wife: Source of Comfort and the Spring of Joy."

One of the most important functions of woman as comforter was her role as nurse. Her own health was probably, although regrettably, delicate. Many homes had "little sufferers," those pale children who wasted away to saintly deaths. And there were enough other illnesses of youth and age, major and minor, to give the nineteenth-century American woman nursing experience. The sickroom called for the exercise of her higher qualities of patience, mercy and gentleness as well as for her housewifely arts. She could thus fulfill her dual feminine function—beauty and usefulness.

The cookbooks of the period offer formulas for gout cordials, ointment for sore nipples, hiccough and cough remedies, opening pills and refreshing drinks for fever, along with recipes for pound cake, jumbles, stewed calves head and currant wine. *The Ladies' New Book of Cookery* believed that "food prepared by the kind hand of a wife, mother, sister, friend" tasted better and had a "restorative power which money cannot purchase."

A chapter of *The Young Lady's Friend* was devoted to woman's privilege as "ministering spirit at the couch of the sick." Mrs. Farrar advised a soft voice, gentle and clean hands, and a cheerful smile. She also cautioned against an excess of female delicacy. That was all right for a young lady in the parlor, but not for bedside manners. Leeches, for example, were to be regarded as "a curious piece of mechanism . . . their ornamental stripes should recommend them even to the eye, and their valuable services to our feelings." And she went on calmly to discuss their use. Nor were women to shrink from medical terminology, since "If you cultivate right views of the wonderful structure of the body, you will be as willing to speak to a physician of the bowels as the brains of your patient."

Nursing the sick, particularly sick males, not only made a woman feel useful and accomplished, but increased her influence. In a piece of heavy-handed humor in *Godey's* a man confessed that some women were only happy when their husbands were ailing that they might have the joy of nursing him to recovery "thus gratifying their medical vanity and their love of power by making him more dependent upon them." In a similar vein a husband sometimes suspected his wife "almost wishes me dead—for the pleasure of being utterly inconsolable."

In the home women were not only the highest adornment of civilization, but they were supposed to keep busy at morally uplifting tasks. Fortunately most of housework, if looked at in true womanly fashion, could be regarded as uplifting. Mrs. Sigourney extolled its virtues: "The science of housekeeping affords exercise for the judgment and energy, ready recollection, and patient self-possession, that are the characteristics of a superior mind." According to Mrs. Farrar, making beds was good exercise, the repetitiveness of routine tasks inculcated patience and perseverance, and proper management of the home was a surprisingly complex art: "There is more to be learned about pouring out tea and coffee, than most young ladies are willing to believe." *Godey's* went so far as to suggest coyly, in "Learning vs. Housewifery" that the two were complementary, not opposed: chemistry could be utilized in cooking, geometry in dividing cloth, and phrenology in discovering talent in children.

Women were to master every variety of needlework, for, as Mrs. Sigourney pointed out, "Needle-work, in all its forms of use, elegance, and ornament, has ever been the appropriate occupation of woman." Embroidery improved taste; knitting promoted serenity and economy. Other forms of artsy-craftsy activity for her leisure moments included painting on glass or velvet, Poonah work, tussy-mussy frames for her own needlepoint or water colors, stands for hyacinths, hair bracelets or baskets of feathers.

She was expected to have a special affinity for flowers. To the editors of *The Lady's Token* "A Woman never appears more truly in her sphere, than when she divides her time between her domestic avocations and the culture of flowers." She could write letters, an activity particularly feminine since it had to do with the outpourings of the heart, or practice her drawingroom skills of singing and playing an instrument. She might even read.

Here she faced a bewildering array of advice. The female was dangerously addicted to novels, according to the literature of the period. She should avoid them, since they interfered with "serious piety." If she simply couldn't help herself and read them anyway, she should choose edifying ones from lists of morally acceptable authors. She should study history since it "showed the depravity of the human heart and the evil nature of sin." On the whole, "religious biography was best."

The women's magazines themselves could be read without any loss of concern for the home. *Godey's* promised the husband that he would find his wife "no less assiduous for his reception, or less sincere in welcoming his return" as a result of reading their magazine. *The Lily of the Valley* won its right to be admitted to the boudoir by confessing that it was "like its namesake humble and unostentatious, but it is yet pure, and, we trust, free from moral imperfections."

No matter what later authorities claimed, the nineteenth century knew that girls *could* be ruined by a book. The seduction stories regard "exciting and dangerous books" as contributory causes of disaster. The man without honorable intentions always provides the innocent maiden with such books as a prelude to his assault on her virtue. Books which attacked or seemed to attack woman's accepted place in society were regarded as equally dangerous. A reviewer of Harriet Martineau's *Society in America* wanted it kept out of the hands of American women. They were so susceptible to persuasion, with their "gentle yielding natures" that they might listen to "the bold ravings of the hard-featured of their own sex." The frightening result: "such reading will unsettle them for their true station and pursuits, and they will throw the world back again into confusion."

The debate over women's education posed the question of whether a "finished" education detracted from the practice of housewifely arts. Again it proved to be a case of semantics, for a true woman's education was never "finished" until she was instructed in the gentle science of homemaking. Helen Irving, writing on "Literary Women," made it very clear that if women invoked the muse, it was as a genie of the household lamp. "If the necessities of her position require these duties at her hands, she will perform them nonetheless cheerfully, that she knows herself capable of higher things." The literary woman must conform to the same standards as any other woman: "That her home shall be made a loving place of rest and joy and comfort for those who are dear to her will be the first wish of every true woman's heart." Mrs. Ann Stephens told women who wrote to make sure they did not sacrifice one domestic duty. "As for genius, make it a domestic plant. Let its roots strike deep in your house. . . ."

The fear of "blue stockings" (the eighteenth-century male's term of derision for educated or literary women) need not persist for nineteenth-century American men. The magazines presented spurious dialogues in which bachelors were convinced of their fallacy in fearing educated wives. One such dialogue took place between a young man and his female cousin. Ernest deprecates learned ladies ("A *Woman* is far more lovable than a *philosopher*") but Alice refutes him with the beautiful example of their Aunt Barbara who "although she *has* perpetrated the heinous crime of writing some half dozen folios" is still a model of "the spirit of feminine gentleness." His memory prodded, Ernest concedes that, by George, there was a woman: "When I last had a cold she not only made me a bottle of cough syrup, but when I complained of nothing new to read, set to work and wrote some twenty stanzas on consumption."

The magazines were filled with domestic tragedies in which spoiled young girls learned that when there was a hungry man to feed French and china painting were not helpful. According to these stories many a marriage is jeopardized because the wife has not learned to keep house. Harriet Beecher Stowe wrote a sprightly piece of personal experience for *Godey's*, ridiculing her own bad housekeeping as a bride. She used the same theme in a story "The Only Daughter," in which the pampered beauty learns the facts of domestic life from a rather difficult source, her mother-in-law. Mrs. Hamilton tells Caroline in the sweetest way possible to shape up in the kitchen, reserving her rebuke for her son: "You are her husband—her guide—her protector—now see what you can do," she admonishes him. "Give her credit for every effort: treat her faults with tenderness; encourage and praise whenever you can, and depend upon it, you will see another woman in her." He is properly masterful, she properly domestic and in a few months Caroline is making lumpless gravy and keeping up with the darning. Domestic tranquillity has been restored and the young wife moralizes: "Bring up a girl to feel that she has a responsible part to bear in promoting the happiness of the family, and you make a reflecting being of her at once, and remove that lightness and frivolity of character which makes her shrink from graver studies." These stories end with the heroine drying her hands on her apron and vowing that *her* daughter will be properly educated, in piecrust as well as Poonah work.

The female seminaries were quick to defend themselves against any suspicion of interfering with the role which nature's God had assigned to women. They hoped to enlarge and deepen that role, but not to change its setting. At the Young Ladies' Seminary and Collegiate Institute in Monroe City, Michigan, the catalogue admitted few of its graduates would be likely "to fill the learned professions." Still, they were called to "other scenes of usefulness and honor." The average woman is to be "the presiding genius of love" in the home, where she is to "give a correct and elevated literary taste to her children, and to assume that influential station that she ought to possess as the companion of an educated man."

At Miss Pierce's famous school in Litchfield, the students were taught that they had "attained the perfection of their characters when they could combine their elegant accomplishments with a turn for solid domestic virtues." Mt. Holyoke paid pious tribute to domestic skills: "Let a young lady despise this branch of the duties of woman, and she despises the appointments of her existence." God, nature and the Bible "enjoin these duties on the sex, and she cannot violate them with impunity." Thus warned, the young lady would have to seek knowledge of these duties elsewhere, since it was not in the curriculum at Mt. Holyoke. "We would not take this privilege from the mother."

One reason for knowing her way around a kitchen was that America was "a land of precarious fortunes," as Lydia Maria Child pointed out in her book *The Frugal Housewife: Dedicated to Those Who Are Not Ashamed of Economy.* Mrs. Child's chapter "How To Endure Poverty" prescribed a combination of piety and knowledge—the kind of knowledge found in a true woman's education, "a thorough religious *useful* education." The woman who had servants today, might tomorrow, because of a depression or panic, be forced to do her own work. If that happened she knew how to act, for she was to be the same cheerful consoler of her husband in their cottage as in their mansion.

An essay by Washington Irving, much quoted in the gift annuals, discussed the value of a wife in case of business reverses: "I have observed that a married man falling into misfortune is more apt to achieve his situation in the world than a single one . . . it is beautifully ordained by Providence that woman, who is the ornament of man in his happier hours, should be his stay and solace when smitten with sudden calamity."

A story titled simply but eloquently "The Wife" dealt with the quiet heroism of Ellen Graham during her husband's plunge from fortune to poverty. Ned Graham said of her: "Words are too poor to tell you what I owe to that noble woman. In our darkest seasons of adversity, she has been an angel of consolation—utterly forgetful of self and anxious only to comfort and sustain me." Of course she had a little help from "faithful Dinah who absolutely refused to leave her beloved mistress," but even so Ellen did no more than would be expected of any true woman.

Most of this advice was directed to woman as wife. Marriage was the proper state for the exercise of the domestic virtues. "True Love and a Happy Home," an essay in *The Young Ladies' Oasis*, might have been carved on every girl's hope chest. But although marriage was best, it was not absolutely necessary. The women's magazines tried to remove the stigma from being an "Old Maid." They advised no marriage at all rather than an unhappy one contracted out of selfish motives. Their stories showed maiden ladies as unselfish ministers to the sick, teachers of the young, or moral preceptors with their pens, beloved of the entire village. Usually the life of single blessedness resulted from the premature death of a fiancé, or was chosen through fidelity to some high mission. For example, in "Two Sisters," Mary devotes herself to Ellen and her abandoned children, giving up her own chance for marriage. "Her devotion to her sister's happiness has met its reward in the consciousness of having fulfilled a sacred duty." Very rarely, a "woman of genius" was absolved from the necessity of marriage, being so extraordinary that she did not need the security or status of being a wife. Most often, however, if girls proved "difficult," marriage and a family were regarded as a cure. The "sedative quality" of a home could be counted on to subdue even the most restless spirits.

George Burnap saw marriage as "that sphere for which woman was originally intended, and to which she is so exactly fitted to adorn and bless, as the wife, the mistress of a home, the solace, the aid, and the counsellor of that ONE, for whose sake alone the world is of any consequence to her." Samuel Miller preached a sermon on women: "How interesting and important are the duties devolved on females as WIVES . . . the counsellor and friend of the husband; who makes it her daily study to lighten his cares, to soothe his sorrows, and to augment his joys; who, like a guardian angel, watches over his interests, warns him against dangers, comforts him under trials; and by her pious, assiduous, and attractive deportment, constantly endeavors to render him more virtuous, more useful, more honourable, and more happy." A woman's whole interest should be focused on her husband, paying him "those numberless attentions to which the French give the title of *petits soins* and which the woman who loves knows so well how to pay . . . she should consider nothing as trivial which could win a smile of approbation from him."

Marriage was seen not only in terms of service but as an increase in authority for woman. Burnap concluded that marriage improves the female character "not only because it puts her under the best possible tuition, that of the affections, and affords scope to her active energies, but because it gives her higher aims, and a more dignified position." *The Lady's Amaranth* saw it as a balance of power: "The man bears rule over his wife's person and conduct. She bears rule over his inclinations: he governs by law; she by persuasion. . . . The empire of the woman is an empire of softness . . . her commands are caresses, her menaces are tears."

Woman should marry, but not for money. She should choose only the high road of true love and not truckle to the values of a materialistic society. A story "Marrying for Money" (subtlety was not the strong point of the ladies' magazines) depicts Gertrude, the heroine, rueing the day she made her crass choice: "It is a terrible thing to live without love. . . . A woman who dares marry for aught but the purest affection, calls down the just judgments of heaven upon her head."

The corollary to marriage, with or without true love, was motherhood, which added another dimension to her usefulness and her prestige. It also anchored her even more firmly to the home. "My Friend," wrote Mrs. Sigourney, "If in becoming a mother, you have reached the climax of your happiness, you have also taken a higher place in the scale of being . . . you have gained an increase of power." The Rev. J. N. Danforth pleaded in *The Ladies' Casket*, "Oh, mother, acquit thyself well in thy humble sphere, for thou mayest affect the world." A true woman naturally loved her children; to suggest otherwise was monstrous.

America depended upon her mothers to raise up a whole generation of Christian statesmen who could say "all that I am I owe to my angel mother." The mothers must do the inculcating of virtue since the fathers, alas, were too busy chasing the dollar. Or as *The Ladies' Companion* put it more effusively, the father "weary with the heat and burden of life's summer day, or trampling with unwilling foot the decaying leaves of life's autumn, has forgotten the sympathies of life's joyous springtime. . . . The acquisition of wealth, the advancement of his children in worldly honor—these are his self-imposed tasks." It was his wife who formed "the infant mind as yet untainted by contact with evil . . . like wax beneath the plastic hand of the mother."

The Ladies' Wreath offered a fifty-dollar prize to the woman who submitted the most convincing essay on "How May An American Woman Best Show Her Patriotism." The winner was Miss Elizabeth Wetherell who provided herself with a husband in her answer. The wife in the essay of course asked her husband's opinion. He tried a few jokes first—"Call her eldest son George Washington," "Don't speak French, speak American"—but then got down to telling her in sober prize-winning truth what women could do for their country. Voting was no asset, since that would result only in "a vast increase of confusion and expense without in the smallest degree affecting the result." Besides, continued this oracle, "looking down at their child," if "we were to go a step further and let the children vote, their first act would be to vote their mothers at home." There is no comment on this devastating male logic and he continues: "Most women would follow the lead of their fathers and husbands," and the few who would "fly off on a tangent from the circle of home influence would cancel each other out."

The wife responds dutifully: "I see all that. I never understood so well before." Encouraged by her quick womanly perception, the master of the house resolves the question—an American woman best shows her patriotism by staying at home, where she brings her influence to bear "upon the right side for the country's weal." That woman will instinctively choose the side of right he has no doubt. Besides her "natural refinement and closeness to God" she has the "blessed advantage of a quiet life" while man is exposed to conflict and evil. She stays home with "her Bible and a well-balanced mind" and raises her sons to be good Americans. The judges rejoiced in this conclusion and paid the prize money cheerfully, remarking "they deemed it cheap at the price."

If any woman asked for greater scope for her gifts the magazines were sharply critical. Such women were tampering with society, undermining civilization. Mary Wollstonecraft, Frances Wright and Harriet Martineau were condemned in the strongest possible language—they were read out of the sex. "They are only semi-women, mental hermaphrodites." The Rev. Harrington knew the women of America could not possibly approve of such perversions and went to some wives and mothers to ask if they did want a "wider sphere of interest" as these nonwomen claimed. The answer was reassuring. " 'NO!' they cried simultaneously, 'Let the men take care of politics, *we will take care of the children!*' " Again female discontent resulted only from a lack of understanding: women were not subservient, they were rather "chosen vessels." Looked at in this light the conclusion was inescapable: "Noble, sublime is the task of the American mother."

"Women's Rights" meant one thing to reformers, but quite another to the True Woman. She knew her rights,

> The right to love whom others scorn,
> The right to comfort and to mourn,
> The right to shed new joy on earth,
> The right to feel the soul's high worth . . .
> Such women's rights, and God will bless
> And crown their champions with success.

The American woman had her choice—she could define her rights in the way of the women's magazines and insure them by the practice of the requisite virtues, or she could go outside the home, seeking other rewards than love. It was a decision on which, she was told, everything in her world depended. "Yours it is to determine," the Rev. Mr. Stearns solemnly warned from the pulpit, "whether the beautiful order of society . . . shall continue as it has been" or whether "society shall break up and become a chaos of disjointed and unsightly elements." If she chose to listen to other voices than those of her proper mentors, sought other rooms than those of her home, she lost both her happiness and her power—"that almost magic power, which, in her proper sphere, she now wields over the destinies of the world."

But even while the women's magazines and related literature encouraged this ideal of the perfect woman, forces were at work in the nineteenth century which impelled woman herself to change, to play a more creative role in society. The movements for social reform, westward migration, missionary activity, utopian communities, industrialism, the Civil War—all called forth responses from woman which differed from those she was trained to believe were hers by nature and divine decree. The very perfection of True Womanhood, moreover, carried within itself the seeds of its own destruction. For if woman was so very little less than the angels, she should surely take a more active part in running the world, especially since men were making such a hash of things.

Real women often felt they did not live up to the ideal of True Womanhood: some of them blamed themselves, some challenged the standard, some tried to keep the virtues and enlarge the scope of womanhood. Somehow through this mixture of challenge and acceptance, of change and continuity, the True Woman evolved into the New Woman—a transformation as startling in its way as the abolition of slavery or the coming of the machine age. And yet the stereotype, the "mystique" if you will, of what woman was and ought to be persisted, bringing guilt and confusion in the midst of opportunity.

The women's magazines and related literature had feared this very dislocation of values and blurring of roles. By careful manipulation and interpretation they sought to convince woman that she had the best of both worlds—power and virtue—and that a stable order of society depended upon her maintaining her traditional place in it. To that end she was identified with everything that was beautiful and holy.

"Who Can Find a Valiant Woman?" was asked frequently from the pulpit and the editorial pages. There was only one place to look for her—at home. Clearly and confidently these authorities proclaimed the True Woman of the nineteenth century to be the Valiant Woman of the Bible, in whom the heart of her husband rejoiced and whose price was above rubies.

Propaganda Uses of the Underground Railroad

LARRY GARA

• The story of the underground railroad in American history
is a popular one. Containing elements of fact, fiction, and
fantasy, it describes how terror-stricken, yet courageous, slaves
made their way North stopping at various "stations" along
their way to freedom. These tales often celebrate and embel-
lish the roles played by numerous white sympathizers and
abolitionists. In the following selection, however, Professor
Larry Gara indicates that many fugitives received aid from
free Negroes, former slaves, and Indians, and that there is
insufficient information available to substantiate the existence of any well-organized underground raliroad. It cannot
be denied that many northern whites helped the fleeing black
men and women but there is also evidence that the blacks
were exploited by their saviors. Propagandists, politicians,
and even wily businessmen sometimes used the erstwhile
bondsmen to serve their own purposes. American historians
have, in the past, placed a great deal of emphasis upon the
humanitarian aspects of the underground railroad but Professor Gara reminds us that it was "far more important as a
propaganda device than as an aid to the fleeing slaves." Gara
also notes that instances of co-operation among fugitive and
fellow blacks and mutual aid societies have not been given
the attention they warrant.

In the years between the opening of the slavery controversy and the
close of the nineteenth century, many people, involved in some way
in aiding fugitive slaves to escape from bondage, wrote articles and
stories relating the thrilling exploits of the humanitarian underground
railroad. Most of these tales followed a fixed pattern, although minor

From *Mid-America*, 34 (July 1952). Reprinted without notes by permission of the author.

variations appeared. With skilled pens, zealous anti-slavery writers painted a picture of frightened fugitives, hotly pursued by vindictive masters and "regular Southern" bloodhounds. The runaways always escaped their would-be captors through the ingenuity and daring of underground railroad "engineers and conductors, ticket agents and train dispatchers," whose secret but "deep laid scheme" of organized aid enabled the erstwhile slaves to wend their way to the freedom-loving North or to "shake the British Lion's paw" beyond the Canadian border.

Despite the mass of romantic and exciting underground railroad literature, the secret organization loomed larger in reminiscence and propaganda than it was in reality. Many fugitives from slavery either refrained from using it or made their escape in ignorance of the facilities the organization provided. When Frederick Douglass left his slave home he borrowed "free papers" from a friendly sailor, and, unaided by abolitionists, traveled North as a free Negro. In 1834, when William Wells Brown escaped from slavery, he supposed "every person" his enemy and "was afraid to appeal to anyone, even for a little food to keep body and soul together." Other fleeing bondsmen also relied upon their own resources and ingenuity. Many traveled alone at night, following the North Star and getting aid from other slaves, free Negroes and Indians. Some of lighter complexion successfully passed as white men. William and Ellen Craft escaped from their Georgia slave home by passing as master and servant. Ellen posed as a young planter badly injured and William acted the part of the faithful servant trying to lead his master to medical attention in the North. The ruse succeeded and the Crafts' imaginative self-help scheme rewarded them with the freedom they sought. Like many other fugitives, the Crafts contacted abolitionists only after they had already escaped from the South. But the numbers who escaped from slavery without any organized assistance did not discourage abolitionist agitators from using the underground stories for propaganda purposes.

In the years immediately preceding the Civil War abolitionist enthusiasts circulated stories of the underground railroad and its line running from slavery to freedom. The combination of courage, adventure and pathos described in the tales was extremely effective, but not all adherents of the abolitionist cause favored the emphasis given underground railroad publicity. In 1855 Frederick Douglass wrote,

"I have never approved of the very public manner in which some of our western friends have conducted what *they* call the '*Under-ground Railroad*,' but which . . . by their open declarations, has been made, most emphatically, the '*Upper*-ground Railroad,'" whose "stations are far better known to the slave holders than to the slaves." Douglass honored the abolitionists for their "noble daring" but questioned the good of so much publicity. "It may," he admitted, "kindle an enthusiasm, very pleasant to inhale; but that is of no practical benefit to themselves, nor to the slaves escaping."

In spite of Douglass' concern, abolitionists continued to publish and spread stories of fugitives' experiences, including detailed expositions of escape methods. The crusaders fully realized the value of such propaganda. "These fugitive stories," wrote an anti-slavery worker, "produced a great effect on all who heard them." The feminine firebrand, Angelina Grimké, admitted to Theodore Weld that while she rejoiced to learn of a recent slave escape, "some of the pleasure was abridged by the caution to keep these things close." She heartily approved of Weld's plan to send the former slave to England and then urged him to publish the "tale of woe," for, she exclaimed, "such narratives are greatly needed, let it come burning from his own lips in England and publish it here. . . . Names, dates and facts will give additional credibility to it. Many and many a tale of romantic horror can the slaves tell."

Her co-workers in the abolition movement heeded Angelina's advice and published many a tale of horror. Some fugitive slave stories had already been published, and in 1838 Whittier's account of the James Williams narrative rolled off the presses. In 1843 Moses Roper's escape story appeared in print. Roper's tale, like most of the early slave narratives, contained no mention of the underground railroad. His was a story of escape without organized aid, although some Southern whites did befriend him as he made his way North.

A steady stream of slave reminiscences followed these first accounts. Literate abolitionists penned the stories of former slaves who could not put their own words into writing. Each new booklet repeated stories of Southern horror and brutality replete with a "foul stream of sexual licentiousness," the "selfishness, . . . cruelty, . . . and profligacy" of the Southern character, and the savagery of "human bloodhounds" conspiring in the "hidden chambers of the dread prison house" to undertake new aggressions against Northern freedom, decency and righteousness. The black picture was only mitigated by a few Southerners, mostly women, "who in secret weep and mourn over the misery and the sin against which they have not the strength thus bravely to protest." The misery and horror of life in the South as pictured in slave accounts was calculated to have a definite effect on Northern readers. One militant abolitionist wrote, "if the publication of such thrilling narratives as this . . . do not rouse the people of the non-slaveholding States . . . not only to withstand the aggressions of these . . . despots, but to break up their tyrannies, then we may look to the day, not distant, when . . . the threat of Senator Douglas, 'we will subdue you,' shall be literally fulfilled, and Senator Toombs may call the roll of his slaves upon Bunker Hill, or the plains of Saratoga."

It was, however, the product of Harriet Beecher Stowe's fertile imagination that proved to be the most important propaganda item inspired by the underground railroad. Written shortly after the passage of the Fugitive Slave Act, *Uncle Tom's Cabin* was an immediate answer. Three hundred thousand copies were printed in one year, and the work soon became popular in Europe where it appeared in numerous translations. Transposed into a drama, Mrs. Stowe's message reached thousands untouched by the book, and the effect was tremendous. "Now melting to tears," wrote Senator Charles Sumner, "and now inspiring to rage, her work everywhere touches the conscience, and makes the slave hunter more hateful." The book molded opinions everywhere in the North, and in the South at least fourteen pro-slavery novels answered its indictment of Southern society. One abolitionist writer rejoiced that "whilst our wise Legislators were fulminating their anathemas against agitation, and solemnly resolving and re-resolving that it should be discountenanced . . . Mrs. Stowe was preparing a firebrand which was to make it blaze with new fury."

Through the medium of slave memoirs and fiction the cruel scenes of the Southern "peculiar institution" soon became familiar in the North. However, the printed word was at best a poor substitute for the living victim, and abolitionists delighted in using the fugitives themselves as propaganda instruments. In 1855 Ohio anti-slavery workers displayed a family of six fugitives, "a specimen of the fruits of the infernal system of slavery." The "surprised and horror-stricken" spectators "generously contributed" money to send the fugitive family on its way to Canada. Levi Coffin, self-styled president of the underground railroad, often exhibited frightened fugitives in his home. He once took a female fugitive to a Quaker Meeting in West Elkton, Indiana. The crusading Coffin later recalled with satisfaction the effectiveness of this technique in raising the morale and extending the operations of the West Elkton abolitionist circle.

The erstwhile slave, Frederick Douglass was a favorite speaker at anti-slavery meetings after 1834, when abolitionists first became convinced that exhibiting "a graduate" of the institution of slavery would make a favorable impression on an audience. Douglass, a powerful speaker and dramatic personality, spoke to numerous audiences in America and England. In Europe he told listeners how he had "to fly from the screeching of the eagle, and take shelter in the lap of the lion." In America Douglass loved to relate his famous slaveholder's sermon based upon the text "servants, be obedient unto your masters." Douglass' manner was proud and his technique effective. According to James Russell Lowell, "the very look and bearing of Douglass are an irresistible logic against the oppression of his race." William Wells Brown also spoke frequently, often reading his own anti-slavery dramas to attentive audiences throughout the North.

Abolitionists fully exploited the propaganda value of former slaves, but these victims were not the only heroes of the underground railroad line. After the passage of the Fugitive Slave Law of 1850, Federal courts increased prosecutions of those who aided escaping slaves. The brave prisoners of conscience who could not appear publicly because of their incarceration for the cause of freedom played an important role in the propaganda war against the ante-bellum South. William M. Connelly's twenty-day ordeal in the Cincinnati jail set off a chain of sympathy demonstrations in his behalf. Women of the city carried to his prison cell fresh-plucked strawberries, hot pies and other delicacies. The Cincinnati public school teachers paraded to the honored convict's abode, and Horace Mann led a group of visiting Unitarians down to the prison to offer spiritual advice and good wishes to the suffering martyr.

Imaginative abolitionists utilized fully the Connelly incident. The climactic event planned by the propagandists was a gala procession and torchlight festival in celebration of Connelly's release from jail. The men planning this colorful event did not realize that Connelly's sentence expired at noon rather than at the evening hour included in their plans. An emergency committee rushed to the jailor who agreed to keep the suffering martyr under lock and key until the proper release demonstration could take place. At the appointed hour, a drenching rain failed to dampen the spirits of the gay crowd. A uniformed band of musicians and several highly decorated carriages bearing men prominent in Cincinnati's Republican Party marched to the jailhouse gates. The procession marched through Cincinnati's German district, for the various German societies played a prominent part in the pageantry. The demonstrators climaxed the evening with a mass meeting at Turner Hall where Connelly spoke of his experiences and effectively discredited Stanley Matthews, the Democratic district attorney who had prosecuted him. Stanley Matthews, who had formerly been a Whig and abolitionist, felt the effects of the Connelly case for a long time afterwards. Political opponents used the incident to defeat him as candidate for Congress in 1876, and later opposed his appointment to the Supreme Court because of the Connelly prosecution. He was finally allowed to sit on the court after 1881, despite the continued efforts of former abolitionists to check his appointment.

In Wisconsin, abolitionists struck a rich vein of publicity in the famous Booth case, which touched off innumerable anti-slavery diatribes and demonstrations. In 1854 a slave owner, with the aid of the sheriff, captured a former slave near Milwaukee and carried him to the local jail. Abolitionists in the area soon learned of the incident and sent word to Sherman M. Booth, an anti-slavery editor in Milwaukee. Booth immediately organized a demonstration, riding through the city shouting: "Freemen! To the rescue! Slave-catchers are in our midst! Be at the court-house at two o'clock!" At the subsequent meeting a mob broke into the jail and released the fugitive, who departed shortly for Canada. Federal authorities charged Booth with aiding and abetting the escape and he received a sentence of one month in prison and a $1,461 fine and costs. The case dragged on in the courts until 1860, when he finally submitted to judicial defeat and entered prison. Refusing to pay his fine, he found himself facing an indeterminate period of imprisonment, but when his friends wished to pay it for him, Booth forbade it, telling them "it would be far more creditable . . . and better for the cause," to give the money to his wife. Futhermore, he refused to ask President Buchanan for a pardon, saying "I think I am doing more here than I could out."

Mass meetings assembled to protest Booth's arrest and imprisonment not only in Wisconsin, but in many Northern communities, for the anti-slavery forces fully capitalized on his case for publicity purposes. In Milwaukee's Young's Hall a state anti-slavery convention passed resolutions against the Fugitive Slave Law and in support of the slave rescuers. Another meeting of enthusiastic abolitionists convened in the same hall to protest Booth's conviction. Still another group passed a resolution calling the Federal judge in the case "an old Granny and a miserable Doughface," while a fourth assembly resolved to help Booth out of his troubles, "if we have to do it at the point of a bayonet." The widespread notice given Wisconsin's Booth case cheered the American Anti-Slavery Society, whose officers felt that "a most sound and healthy tone of feeling appears to have pervaded that youthful Commonwealth."

Another widely publicized underground railroad incident was the famed Oberlin-Wellington Rescue, in which Ohio abolitionists rescued a fugitive slave from a United States Marshal in Wellington, Ohio. In December of 1858 the Federal government indicted thirty-seven alleged accomplices under the Fugitive Slave Law and their legal fight gave signal to a series of demonstrations, sympathy rallies and political meetings throughout Ohio. When the Oberlin abolitionists left for their trial in Cleveland, a cheering crowd gathered at the Oberlin station to bid them farewell. In Cleveland a widely publicized "felon's feast" honored the crusaders. Sympathetic spectators packed the courtroom during the trial and cheered the defendants' strong statements. None of the abolitionists served more than eighty-five days in prison, but while they paced cells in Cleveland jail their fellow workers made good use of their martyrdom. Large gatherings enabled Ohio citizens to learn of the righteousness of the abolition cause and the Republican Party. The largest of the meetings was held on May 24, 1859, in Cleveland, where various Republican leaders gave "stirring speeches." One orator told the crowd that "the Democracy of this day is opposed to civil and religious liberty." Another advised the ladies in the audience to influence their men folk to vote the "slavocracy" out of power. They should, he advised, tell their husbands and lovers "to go to the polls and do their duty, then come back and claim their reward."

Oberlin sympathizers held meetings in the summer of 1859. By this time, partisan lines divided public reaction to underground railroad propaganda. Republican politicians took credit for underground railroad activity, and newspapers generally slanted underground stories to fit their political bias. A Democratic editor from Cleveland referred to the "rebellious Higher Law creed" of Oberlin's "myrmidons of Mormonism," and other Ohio Democrats called the four naturalized Britishers among the rescuers the "Oberlin Jacks and Donkeys." After government officials released the Oberlin rescuers, Republican editors printed stories of a magnificent "triumph" for "Freedom," and a "disastrous defeat" for those who had tried to enforce the Fugitive Slave Law.

When the last Oberlin prisoner left his cell in July of 1859, local abolitionists prepared more gigantic demonstrations. In the small Ohio village one hundred guns saluted his return and abolitionists held a mass meeting in a crowded church. Meanwhile ambitious antislavery workers collected materials for a book based on the Oberlin case. The volume went to press barely a week after the last Oberlin martyr left prison, and readers of Garrison's *Liberator* were told to "Read it . . . and MOURN over your country's degradation; scatter it broadcast over the land, that a SLAVOCRATIC NATION may see the depth of depravity and wickedness into which it has fallen, and arouse, repent and reform." Anti-slavery propagandists were not unhappy about the Oberlin martyrs. One wrote in retrospect concerning the case, "It stimulated discussion, roused popular feeling, extended and deepened the abhorrence felt toward slave catching . . . and called forth many an emphatic utterance of that sentiment from pulpit, and press, and public meeting, and so helped on the preparation of the public mind for the inevitable death-grapple with the Slavepower, toward which all events are surely drifting us."

Unfortunately, not all individuals involved in underground railroad work were as unselfish as the Fugitive Slave Law martyrs. Some people found a source of income in underground railroad activities. Avaricious boat captains running north from Southern ports profiteered on slaves desiring to escape from their drudgery. When a group of abolitionists hired Daniel Drayton to arrange for the escape of a group of slaves from Washington they included in his expense account one hundred dollars to pay for the hire of a boat. The captain of the *Pearl* offered the use of his vessel for this illegal purpose since the amount offered was "considerably more than the vessel could earn in any ordinary trip of the like duration." Another profit-conscious boat captain made it his business to circulate underground railroad stories to the unfortunates held in Southern bondage. He contrasted an alluring picture of Northern freedom with the unremunerated monotony of slave toil. The Fugitive Slave Law, he told his slave listeners, did not apply to the Northern States. His encouragement to find a haven in the North stimulated at least one unsuspecting Negro to pay the captain two hundred dollars, only to find himself in Boston without aid or friends in view. "The moment the vessel touched the wharf, the scoundrel bade the poor fellow be off in a moment; and he then discovered his liability to be pursued and taken."

Alleged agents of the free Negro colonies in Canada sometimes swindled humanitarian anti-slavery workers. In 1833 the inhabitants of the Wilberforce free Negro colony warned anti-slavery workers not to give any contributions to their former agent, Israel Lewis, who had proved untrustworthy. A member of the colony later lamented that the dishonest agent "collected money professedly for the assistance of the colony" but "would neither pay it over, . . . nor give any account of his proceedings. Very little did he ever pay over to the aid of the colony as designed."

Abolitionists, fugitives, and wily profiteers were not the only ones to benefit from underground railroad propaganda. A thorough knowledge of the underground railroad stories provided excellent emotional ammunition for beggars. In 1855 a bogus fugitive received aid from New York abolitionists before they discovered her to be an imposter. Anti-slavery workers printed the story in their newspaper and warned their readers that "we hear very frequently of cases of imposture under pretence of having run away from slavery. Sympathy with fugitives is now so general that dishonest colored persons often succeed in getting pretty liberal supplies of clothes and money without running any serious hazard of detection and exposure."

A year later a Detroit abolitionist told the story of one man who made a practice of traveling through the country begging, "sometimes to buy himself, and at other times his family." He described the fake fugitive carefully, and cautioned abolitionists against accepting any signed credentials the dissembler might present. "Fluent in speech, fully calculated to take advantage of many persons," this imposter went from house to house in some neighborhoods and managed to collect "a considerable amount" of money. Philadelphia anti-slavery workers also encountered pretended underground railroad passengers, and in New England the Quaker abolitionist, Elizabeth Chace, met with two imposters who profited from her anti-slavery sentiments. One of them was an escapee from a nearby prison whom the State authorities later apprehended. While at the Chace household, the would-be fugitive "made himself very interesting and agreeable to us during his stay, by his stories of southern life, by his elegant manners, and especially by his great desire to learn about our ideas of right and wrong."

Not all of the ante-bellum uses of the underground railroad propaganda were illegitimate. Henry Bibb, the Negro colonizer and journalist, used underground railroad stories extensively in his paper, *The Voice of The Fugitive*, published in Sandwich, Ontario. Bibb delighted in printing these lurid tales and used them to raise money for his Canadian colony as well as to add punch and color to the publication. Bibb pointed his journalistic shouts of defiance at the Southern institution. In his paper dated November 5, 1851, he boasted, "we can run a lot of slaves through from almost any of the bordering slave states into Canada within 48 hours and we defy the slaveholders and their abettors to beat that if they can."

Southern slave owners were not the only ones to be disturbed by Bibb's rantings. In 1853 an enraged incendiary started a fire which destroyed the Bibb press. This occasioned an extra edition of the abolitionist sheet informing readers of the decision to go on with the publication, appealing for funds, and relating the latest news of the underground railroad. Although limited space somewhat cramped Bibb's style, he briefly noted, concerning underground operations, "the cry is, still they come, from all parts of the Southern States."

Spokesmen for the Southern cause accepted the stories of Bibb and the abolitionists at face value and answered them. One Louisville editor claimed that "the operation of the Underground railroad and the certainty of escape when once the line is passed, take from 1500 to 2000 slaves from this State alone each year." Another ante-bellum editor complained that "the northern fanatics have so systematized their efforts to steal our slaves, have so organized their underground railroad, that it is impossible for individuals, however vigilant, to frustrate their designs." Many an editor culled underground railroad files for material to clinch a partisan argument. A South Carolinian argued against recognition of Lincoln's election by labeling the Republican administration one "whose creed it is, to repeal the Fugitive Slave laws," and whose object was to transform the underground railroad into an "*overground* railroad."

The Southern response to underground railroad propaganda constituted another phase of the ideological war between the sections which preceded the armed conflict. However, it was in the post-war period that abolitionist writers produced the great wealth of underground railroad literature. Dipping their pens in the blood of the recent conflict, these venerable crusaders recorded youthful deeds of heroism and daring.

William Still, a Negro active for many years in the work of the Philadelphia Vigilance Committee, wrote one of the first books on the underground railroad. Still's work became a major source book for later writers and historians, many of whom repeated his stories in their own writings. It was Still's avowed intention to give his readers only "simple facts" with no resort to "coloring to make the book seem romantic." Despite his proclaimed objectivity, Still informed his readers that "those who come after us seeking for information in regard to the existence, atrocity, struggles and destruction of Slavery, will have no trouble in finding this many-headed monster ruling and tyrannizing over Church and State, North and South, white and black, without hindrance for several generations. Nor will posterity have any difficulty in finding the deeds of the brave and invincible foes of slavery."

William Still wrote about cruel and abusive masters who drank excessively, gambled frequently, and delighted in whipping naked slave girls. Still's data came from the files of the Philadelphia Vigilance Committee. The members of this group carefully questioned each former slave who needed its financial assistance. The committee's preference for libertine masters nearly deprived one needy fugitive of the necessary aid for a trip to Canada. This honest woman claimed that she was "used very well" and "had it good all her life." Her adamance "somewhat staggered the faith of the Committee, but they could not dispute her testimony, consequently they gave her the benefit of the doubt."

Not all of the applicants for aid from the Vigilance Committee were oblivious to the prejudices of the group. One hardy fellow told the thrilled committee of the life and death struggle which preceded his escape. The slave's enraged master gave him twenty blows on the head with the butt of a cowhide, beat him with a shovel until the handle split, and then stabbed him across the stomach and about the head, after which he managed to escape and run for sixteen miles carrying part of his entrails in his hands "for the whole journey." Another destitute fugitive told the committee that he lived three months in a cave "surrounded with bears, wild cats, rattlesnakes and the like."

The methods used by Still to gather evidence for his story were scientific compared with those of most abolitionist writers. The aging zealots perceived events dimly through the passing years and recorded with further embellishment the exaggerated stories of their ante-bellum predecessors. Levi Coffin used his diary and some other remaining documents plus his memory when writing his reminiscences in 1880. The seventy-eight year old abolitionist admitted that errors were destined to appear in his writing because of his advanced age. Another writer, a descendant of abolitionists, deplored the passing of underground railroad workers, and confessed difficulty in distinguishing fact from fiction. This historian admitted the necessity for reliance "largely on tradition for a history of those stirring days." The Quaker Robert C. Smedley visited aged participants and added their recollections to his own in his history of the underground railroad.

The post-war writers of the underground railroad used failing memories and hearsay to concoct their versions of the institution. The writers were all Northern and most of them were connected in some way with the abolitionist movement. Their stories repeated the same sectional hatred, glamorized adventures, and stereotypes which characterized the accounts of ante-bellum writers. The post-war crusaders introduced a new theme into the literature, however. Revered and respected abolitionists recalled to the minds of their readers the unpopularity of abolitionists in the earlier period and the hardships involved in the crusader's life. The white-haired writers of anti-slavery reminiscences delighted in reminding posterity of the vindication of their cause. With quivering pen one of these battle-worn knights wrote "we must concede that it required the manhood of a man, and the unflinching fortitude of a woman, upheld by a full and firm Christian faith, to be an abolitionist in those days, and especially an Underground Railroad agent."

Another elderly crusader wrote "the friends of liberty" were only "invigorated by . . . persecution, . . . and the great upheaval advanced constantly as the people were informed. Violent hostility was thus the means of keeping up the agitation against itself; agitation led to information and thought, and that to constant enlistment and progress." In 1884 Williams Wells Brown evaluated the abolitionists' characters for the benefit of a commemorative meeting of former anti-slavery workers. Brown, who could not attend the meeting, sent a letter telling the aging reformers that "for moral courage, self-sacrifice, indomitable will, true magnetism, patient waiting, and sublime eloquence, these men and women were without a parallel in the world's history of reformers." The aged abolitionists nodded with approval when, at the same meeting, another speaker reminded them "how the darkness of that period was dissipated in the brightness of the emancipation morning! The present generation . . . cannot know what it was to be an abolitionist in the country's 'Martyr Age.' "

Rambling old folks were not the only ones to write and speak of underground railroad activities in the post-war period. Local historians in the Northern states wrote with pride of the role of their sections in the underground epic. Every barn that had ever housed a fugitive became an underground railroad station in post-war histories. "Almost every hamlet" in Ohio, wrote one local historian, "had at least one station." Another writer of county history apologetically explained the lack of underground railroad tradition in his area by a dearth of abolitionists there. A Wisconsin antiquarian related in detail one escape episode and then told his readers that the incident offered proof that an underground railroad ranch "ran through the eastern part of Walworth County." Another historian boasted of the early date when fugitive slaves found refuge and help in his Ohio county. One writer gave clear indication of Pennsylvania's pride in her underground railroad history when he wrote, "the Underground Railroad was but one of the instruments used by the state in her long warfare against slavery, a warfare so aggressive as to distinguish her above all of her sister commonwealths."

The post-war popularity of the underground railroad was amply demonstrated by the writers who made political capital of it. One partisan historian reminded his readers that "but for the Republican party, our own free soil would still be hunting ground for the harassed fugitives from slavery. This very ground would be cursed with the tread of hunters for human chattels. Such is what the Democratic party would have made our whole country to this day and forever." The same writer reluctantly admitted that some who were Democrats until "the Democratic party fired on the old flag at Sumter," had also aided in the underground railroad work. He noted with satisfaction, however, that these individuals had repented of their political past and stated: "I do not know a man from whom we ever received aid and comfort in this enterprise, who is now in that party." A milder author with similar political views told of a slave who received aid from a "pro-slavery Democrat, [who] notwithstanding his politics" was a "soul of honor, and possessed a great and generous heart." The Republican party did not have a monopoly on underground railroad writers. Another historian with definite political convictions carefully pointed out that in one of his experiences a load of fugitives was "carried to Canada concealed in the hold of a sailing vessel by a lake captain, then and now a robust Democrat in politics, a man with a conscience and a heart."

The post-war political uses of the underground railroad stories attest to their widespread popularity and acceptance. Another indication of their popular appeal was the use made of this literature by James Williams, an itinerant California book peddler who went from town to town towards the end of the nineteenth century selling his story of underground railroad escape. The semi-literate Williams titled his booklet *The Life and Adventures of James Williams a Fugitive Slave with a Full Description of the Underground Railroad*. The book, which went into at least five editions, sold for fifty cents and contained comments on issues of the day ranging from Mormonism to a defense of the Chinese immigrants, all equally unintelligible. The readable sections of Williams' work recounted old stories of the underground railroad. These the author lifted verbatim from the book by William Still, and interspersed them with his own confused comments.

Whether underground railroad writers told their tales to recall the days of heroic deeds, to lend aid to the political party of their preference, or merely to sell a book, all used material of an unreliable nature. The combination of dimmed memories, partial sources, and partisan motives mingled truth and fiction in these accounts. Because of the often repeated underground railroad story, written from the abolitionist vantage point, historians have exaggerated this phase of the drama and have given little attention to the story of the fugitives' self-help and mutual aid in their heroic struggle for freedom. The wealth of underground railroad literature gives clear title to its importance, but the institution was far more important as a propaganda device than as an aid to the fleeing slaves. One abolitionist writer with a less exalted view of the underground railroad wrote, "it is said by the poet that 'distance lends enchantment to the view'; and in regard to the escape of fugitive slaves by what was called the 'Underground Railroad,' I am convinced that the number passing over this line has been greatly magnified in the long period of time since this road ceased to run its always irregular trains."

Why the Southern States Seceded

AVERY O. CRAVEN

• The Civil War is the central event in the domestic history of the United States. Measured in terms of loss of life, property damage, and enduring bitterness it was the costliest of all American wars. The surrender at Appomattox of Robert E. Lee's Army of Northern Virginia ended the armed rebellion. But it represented more than battlefield accomplishment; it signaled the ascendancy of industrialism over agriculture, of the city over the farm, and of centralized authority over states' rights. Charles A. Beard called it the "Second American Revolution."

Most of the men who died in the struggle probably had no clear commitment either to abolition or to slavery; General Robert E. Lee himself refused to defend either slavery or secession. Why then did the war come? Was it the moral question posed by involuntary servitude, or was it a constitutional question relating to the powers reserved for the federal government? Or was it the inevitable result of irresistible economic forces? The question has puzzled politicians and scholars for over a century. No one has wrestled longer with the causes of the American Civil War than Avery Craven, who spent most of his professional life teaching American history at the University of Chicago. In the following essay Professor Craven conveys a deep sense of the human aspects of the fateful decision to break apart the Union.

On December 14, 1860, a conservative Georgia editor stated in terms, which he evidently supposed everyone would understand and accept, the reasons why the southern states were seceding from the Union. "It is a mistake," he said, "to suppose that it is the mere election of Lincoln, without regard to anything else, that has driven the States of the South into their present resistance, and their present determination to seek that safety and security out of the Union which they have been unable to obtain within it."

What that "anything else" was, he then made clear. "The election of Lincoln," he said, "is merely the confirmation of a purpose which the South had hoped would be abandoned by the opponents of slavery in the North. It is a declaration that they mean to carry out their aggressive and destructive policy, weakening the institution at every point where it can be assailed either by legislation or by violence, until, in the brutal language of Charles Sumner, 'it dies like a poisoned rat in its hole.' "

The things to be noticed in this bald statement are that northern aggression consisted primarily in the determination to put the institution of Negro slavery on the road to ultimate extinction; that Lincoln's election made the carrying-out of that policy both possible and probable; and that the southern states, much against their wills, had been forced to seek "that safety and security" for their peculiar institution, outside the Union, which they had a perfectly good constitutional right to expect within it.

Most Southerners agreed that Republican hostility to slavery and the evidence of wide northern approval in Lincoln's election justified secession. They somehow felt that the real question before the people in the recent election had not been whether Breckinridge or Lincoln, Bell or Douglas, should be President but whether slavery be perpetuated or abolished. As one writer said: "No man of common sense, who is not prepared to surrender the institution of slavery with the safety and independence of the South can doubt that the time for action has come—now or never!" Some saw the economic danger ahead. "It was not safe," they said, "to trust eight hundred million dollars worth of negroes in the hands of a power that says we do not own the property, that the title under the Constitution is bad, and under the law of God still worse. . . . Slave property is the foundation of all property in the South. When security in this is shaken, all other property partakes of its instability."

Others objected to the Republican boast of moral superiority. They placed "honor" above "interest." They resented less what the Republicans had done or might do, than the things they said and the self-righteous way in which they said them. They could shrug off the material threats, but they could no longer endure the "untiring efforts" to degrade the South in the eyes of all who came within their reach—denying the piety of their clergy, and calling their congressmen "desperadoes" less worthy of trust than "the inmates of our penitentiaries." The question of honor was "paramount to all others."

But more than abstract honor was involved. Republican victory in 1860 was not just a temporary slip. The South had fallen steadily behind the North in population and, denied expansion, was losing political equality as well. The Republican threat to a way of life was bad enough. To lose all hope of an equal voice in national affairs was even worse. As one desperate Southerner said: "Rather than to surrender Southern equality in the Union, let our slaves be lost . . . our fields be desolated . . . our blood to flow," but "never, never should her people . . . yield this most precious of all earthly possessions—their feeling of self-respect."

The official statements made by the seceding conventions in their appeal to the rest of mankind for a sympathetic understanding of their "momentous step" also stressed first of all the threat to their "domestic institutions." The election of a sectional President, "pledged to principles and a policy which we regard as repugnant to the Constitution . . . beget[s] a feeling of insecurity which . . . alarm[s] a people jealous of their rights." The southern states were now a helpless minority "in imminent peril, being in the power of a majority, reckless of Constitutional obligations and pledged to principles leading to [their] destruction."

Some complained of the exclusion of their citizens from territories "owned in common by all the States" and of northern approval of John Brown's raid, but the one grievance above all others was the refusal to return fugitive slaves. This refusal proved beyond all doubt that neither the Constitution of the United States nor the Acts of Congress nor the decisions of the Supreme Court could longer be relied upon as protection for southern rights.

The final, and perhaps the most powerful emotional factor in the situation, was brought out by a speaker in the Alabama Convention.

Mr. President, if pecuniary loss alone were involved in the abolition of slavery, I should hesitate long to give the vote I now intend to give. If the destruction of slavery entailed on us poverty alone, I could bear it, for I have seen poverty and felt its sting. But poverty, Mr. President, would be one of the least of evils that would befall us from the abolition of African slavery. There are now in the slaveholding states over four million slaves; dissolve the relation of master and slave, and what, I ask, would become of that race? To remove them from among us is impossible. History gives us no account of the exodus of such a number of persons. We neither have a place to which to remove them, nor the means of such removal. They, therefore, must remain with us; and if the relation of master and slave be dissolved, and our slaves be turned loose amongst us without restraint, they would either be destroyed by our own hands—the hands to which they look, and look with confidence for protection—or we ourselves would become demoralized and degraded.

Nor was there any reason to hope that the war on slavery would ever cease. As one editor put it:

The settled hostility of the Northern people must become stronger with each year. The present dominant party in the Free States, based upon the single idea of opposition to the extension, spread, or existence of slavery, now numbering in its ranks nearly two million voters, will become more powerful as the sentiment upon which it is founded gains strength and intensity. It has now secured the President. In two years more, at most, it will have both Houses of Congress. Then the Supreme Court will be reorganized . . . and we shall have "no more Dred Scott decisions."

As the Reverend Benjamin M. Palmer told his people: "A whole generation has been educated to look upon the system of slavery with abhorrence as a national blot. They hope, and look, and pray for its extinction within a reasonable time, and cannot be satisfied unless things are seen drawing to that conclusion." It had thus become perfectly clear that the North either "could not let slavery alone," or "would not" or did not "intend to let it alone." It was just as clear, they said, that the "Black Republican victory of November [was] incontrovertible proof of a diseased and dangerous public opinion all over the North, and a certain forerunner of further and more atrocious aggression."

There had been serious crises in national affairs at other times, and Southerners had, more than once, threatened secession. But never before had there been such an atmosphere of desperation and finality, such intense realization of impending disaster, such a feeling of helplessness in the face of what seemed to be a driving force against which resistance had all along been hopeless. Lincoln's election did not present an immediate threat, but it did indicate that a new and final stage in the slavery struggle had been reached. Seemingly the nation had got itself into such a predicament that no one, however well meaning, could check the drift toward the use of force.

Up until the John Brown raid, there had been much southern protest and indignation because of northern criticism of slavery and because of denial of equality in the territories and in the distribution of governmental favors. But there had been little panic and much confidence in the southern politician's ability to protect his section, confidence in northern friends and in the Democratic party. Now all was changed. Talk of the "irrepressible conflict" and of "the higher law" now meant something. The Republican party, a strange mixture of moral values and sectional economic interests, had triumphed in a national election. Stephen A. Douglas had been forced to interpret his squatter-sovereignty doctrine in accordance with the views of his northern supporters, and the South's desperate gamble at Charleston to control the Democratic party, to secure federal protection of slavery in the territories, and to force the northern Democracy back under southern control, had failed. The game had been lost, and submission or secession were the only choices left.

For the first time the Southerner had to face the serious realities of life in a slaveholding society. He had to recognize the possibility of ultimate emancipation. He had to calculate the financial risk of having millions of dollars invested in slaves swept away; face the frightening possibility of bloody racial readjustment; be content with permanent political impotence if three-fifths of his slaves were no longer counted as population; and, above all, accept the harsh, cold fact that he stood alone in a world which insisted that slavery was both an economic burden and a moral outrage.

Other issues now lost their importance. Every decision had to be made according to the demands of slavery, and slavery alone. The only defense against economic, social, and political ruin lay in placing slavery beyond the reach of its enemies. The South had been driven into a corner. The choice between submission and secession would have to be made sooner or later.

Abraham Lincoln had understood the southern dilemma and had talked of solving the economic difficulty by compensated emancipation, and the social-racial problem by removing the Negro from the country. He had once framed a bill for these purposes. But nothing had come from his thinking, and the Republican threat, in southern eyes, was the old abolition threat to deal with slavery as a sin to be removed by the usual revival technique of conviction, repentance, and voluntary and immediate renunciation. The resulting problems were not to be taken into consideration.

The idea that some concessions or some plan such as Lincoln had suggested might have saved the day even at this late date overlooks two important considerations. At no time after the early 1830's is there a single shred of evidence to show that any number of planters, intoxicated by the notion that "Cotton was King," would have surrendered a single slave for any consideration ever suggested. It was now too late, even if it had once been possible—which is doubtful. Nor would the abolitionist at any time have considered such a proposal. As one editor put it: "The disease is too deep seated. The election of Mr. Lincoln to the Presidency, gives a tremendous onward impulse to anti-slavery sentiment. He rides a wave he cannot control or guide to conservative results, even if so disposed."

The historian attempting to answer the question as to why the southern states seceded must recognize the predicament into which the nation had fallen. He must understand that the southern states were right when they said that their domestic institutions were no longer safe in the Union. They erred only in not recognizing the more important fact that their institutions were not safe anywhere in the nineteenth century and the emerging Modern World. They were blind, also, in not realizing that secession was no remedy for their troubles in this age of growing national consolidation. They would find out, after four bloody years of heroic fighting, that in this age organization, efficiency, technology, and urban industrialism win wars regardless of individual courage and sacrifice.

The historian must also understand that Lincoln, in turn, was toying with the impossible when he said that slavery, where it existed, would be safe under his administration. He could not have checked the agitation against slavery, nor could he have guaranteed the return of fugitive slaves. He should have known that in the United States an institution which he himself had said was morally wrong could not longer be legally right. William H. Seward showed a far better understanding of the Republican party when he insisted that all human law "must be brought to the standard of the law of God . . . and must stand or fall by it." Charles Sumner saw the situation more clearly than either Lincoln or Seward when he said:

> They have proclaimed slavery to be *wrong*, and have pledged themselves with force against its extension. It is difficult to sense how they can longer sustain themselves *merely* on that grounds. Their promise sustains a broader conclusion, that is, the duty of no longer allowing the *continuance* of evil anywhere within our Constitutional action. They must become Abolitionists.

The abolitionists themselves had understood this and had resolved that the Republican position on "the folly and wrong of slavery," from which they drew "only the modest inference" that it ought not to be allowed to spread, really implied that "it ought not to be tolerated anywhere." It should also be recalled that both Seward and Lincoln had brought the moral issue into politics and used it to advance their political fortunes. Seward had talked of "the higher law" and "the irrepressible conflict," and Lincoln had insisted on the necessity of opposing Stephen A. Douglas, practical politician, because Douglas had been foolish enough to say that he did not care whether the people of a territory voted slavery up or down, even though he knew and Lincoln knew that they would vote it down. In so doing, they had lifted the issue to the abstract level of right versus wrong and had thereby created a situation with which the democratic process of toleration and compromise could not deal. Only force would answer.

With this much accepted, the historian must then remember that the final centering on antislavery aggression as the sum total of southern complaints was only the last stage in a long series of developments. Somewhere in the years after 1815, the South began taking over from the North the role of "the abused." In the emerging era when progress was beginning to be measured in terms of industry, cities, and complex finances, some southern spokesmen saw the inevitable growth of federal power and the corresponding decline of the agricultural South. They foresaw the day when the South would be reduced to that colonial status described, in 1860, as one in which "Yankees" monopolized "the carrying trade with its immense profits," "all the importing," and "most of the exporting business for the whole Union." "New York City, like a mighty queen of commerce, sits proudly upon her island throne, sparkling in jewels and waving an undisputed commercial scepter over the South. By means of her railways and navigable streams, she sends out her long arms to the extreme South, and with avidity rarely equaled, grasps our gains and transfers them to herself—taxing us at every step—and depleting us as extensively as possible without actually destroying us."

And the reason for this, they charged, was that "the whole policy of the Federal Government, from the beginning [had] been to build up and enrich the North at Southern expense. In this business, the monster engine, a high Protective Tariff, [had] been the chief instrument." And besides this, there had been the "fishing bounties, and the navigation laws, and the giving away the public lands, millions of acres at a time, all of which tend[ed] to aggrandise the Northern section of the Union." "On every living issue deemed vital to the South," said the Charleston *Mercury*, "the Northern members, as a body, [have been] against the South."

John Taylor of Caroline, in Virginia, had early talked this way, and Robert Turnbull, in South Carolina, had brought it to a climax in nullification days. Both denounced the tariff and the "consolidation" trends which permitted its passage. Both viewed it as a violation of the Constitution and as a conflict between economic interests. As Turnbull wrote in denouncing the tariff as "the recent exercise of powers never contemplated by the framers of the Constitution, . . . the more National and less Federal the Government becomes, the more certainly will the interests of the great majority of the states be promoted, but with the same certainty, will the interests of the

South be depressed and destroyed." The interest of the North and West was "that the Government should become more and more National," while the interest of the South was "that it should continue Federal."

For this reason northern statesmen were "not astute to enquire" as to whether an act was in keeping with "the clear intent and meaning of the Constitution." They did not tremble at such violations. Only the South had an interest in checking unconstitutional acts and in keeping the nation federal in character.

Thus for its interests and its safety, Turnbull insisted that the South must forever oppose the implied powers of Congress. The interests of the North and West would always lead them toward "usurpation" and departure from the social compact. They had no reason to quarrel with an expanding national government which was building *their* industry with unconstitutional tariffs, and *their* commerce with unconstitutional internal improvements. Bitterly Turnbull noted that "we hear of no projects in Congress to tax the manufactures of the North to support the agriculture of the South." It was all the other way around.

Alexis de Tocqueville, too, had seen such a situation as marking the end of our federal system. "States form confererations," he wrote, "in order to derive equal advantages from their union. . . . If one of the federated states acquire a preponderance sufficiently great to enable it to take exclusive possession of the central authority, it will . . . cause its own supremacy to be respected under the name of the sovereignty of the Union. Great things may then be done in the name of the Federal Government, but in reality that Government will have ceased to exist."

The tariff, however, in spite of its sectional character, poorly explained the growing inferiority and colonial status of the South as a section. Nor could southern unity be secured in opposition. Too many Southerners were longing for a diversified economic life, and too many saw other reasons for the South's plight. "Why are we so far behind in the great march of improvement?" asked one citizen. "Simply because we have failed to act in obedience to the dictates of sound policy. Simply because we have been almost criminally neglectful of our own interests." "You may nullify the tariff," said another, "but you cannot nullify the fertile soils of Alabama and Mississippi."

And so the tariff issue lost much of its appeal with the failure of nullification. South Carolina had stood alone. Her warning to the South had been in vain. In time, the industrialists of the North and the planters of the South would join hands in shaping the nation's tariff schedules.

In the meantime, John C. Calhoun, unabashed and unenlightened by his nullification experience, had taken up where Turnbull left off. In the early 1830's he had come forward with the assertion that Negro slavery, as practiced in the South, was "a positive good." He followed this, in 1837, with what was ultimately to become the fatal southern orthodox platform. In a series of resolutions offered in the Senate, December 27, he insisted on the strictly federal character of the government in which the states had retained their sovereignty and "the exclusive and sole right over their own domestic institutions and police"; that "any meddling of any one or more States, or a combination of their citizens, with the domestic institutions and police of the others, on any grounds, or under any pretext whatever, political, moral or religious, with a view to their alteration or subversion, is an assumption of superiority, not warranted by the Constitution:—insulting to the States interfered with,—tending to endanger their domestic peace and tranquility."

This government, he said, had been founded to give increased stability and security to the domestic institutions of the states, and since slavery was such a southern institution, "no change of opinion or feeling, on the part of other states . . . in relation to it, can justify them or their citizens in open and systematic attacks thereon, with a view to its overthrow." He closed with the assertion that efforts to abolish slavery in the District of Columbia on the pretext "that it is immoral or sinful" would be an attack on the institutions of all slaveholding states, while the effort to check its expansion into the territories would be a denial of southern equality in the Union.

Here was an implied ultimatum to the effect that the permanence of the Union depended on the universal acceptance of the sovereignty of the states in a federal system and of the positive good of Negro slavery above criticism. It was a demand which men who had caught stride with the oncoming Modern World, even though not yet clearly conscious of its full meaning, could not possibly accept. It would, however, cause them to pause and to think, and instinctively to resist. Interests and morals were both involved.

Calhoun's extreme demands and his blindness or indifference to the nationalistic and democratic-humanitarian character of the age in which he lived had exactly the opposite effects from those he had intended. Already his short-sighted efforts to check antislavery petitions had enabled John Quincy Adams to bring a sacred American right to the support of the hitherto rather ineffective abolition movement. His next equally rash and short-sighted move to annex Texas solely on grounds of safety to southern institutions linked slavery and expansion, pushed the issue into politics, and created the impression that there was a "slave power" bent on spreading its peculiar institution. by every means possible to every corner of the nation. Its ultimate purpose was just "to lug new slave states in" and thereby gain political control. A new and wider antislavery appeal was thus available; its political possibilities greatly expanded.

Calhoun and his supporters, it would seem, were bent on proving true all that the abolitionists had charged. By not understanding the fact that they were fighting an age, not just a group of fanatics, they had alarmed and aroused the whole North. Joshua Giddings in Congress was thereby enabled, with wide approval, to charge that the North was "politically bound, hand and foot, surrendered to the rule and government of a slave-holding oligarchy." He could insist, with equal support, that "Our tariff is as much an anti-slavery measure as the rejection of Texas. So is the subject of internal improvements and the distribution of the proceeds of the public lands. The advocates of perpetual slavery oppose all of them, they regard them as opposed to the interests of slavery." Blundering southern leadership had thus placed their section squarely across the path of what northern men had begun to think of as progress. They were demanding that the world stand still.

When James K. Polk, Democrat and slaveholder, accepted war with Mexico but compromised the Oregon boundary, fostered a lower tariff, and vetoed a river and harbor bill aimed primarily to aid the West, the North was ready with the Wilmot Proviso to check proslavery gains in the new territories. The sectional struggle shifted sharply from slavery per se to one of slavery expansion, and the bitter sectional crisis which quickly developed revealed the tragic condition into which the nation had fallen. A southern movement, impossible before, spontaneously developed, and the call went out for a southern convention. Talk of secession became common, and the charge of northern disregard for the Constitution and northern determination to monopolize the territories as a means of abolishing slavery accepted without question. On the other side, northern determination to check the spread of slavery and an awakened consciousness of slavery as a national disgrace were as marked and as positive.

The frantic efforts of patriots finally shifted the issues from abstractions to the concrete problems involved, and compromise became possible. But secession did not come until Calhoun had again proclaimed the sovereignty of the states; had restated his charge of northern aggression; and had made his demands for equal rights in the territories, the end of slavery agitation, the faithful observance of fugitive slave laws, and constitutional amendments to restore sectional equilibrium. He demonstrated again the fact that southern leadership had remained largely untouched and unchanged by the facts and thoughts of the onrushing nineteenth century.

William H. Seward, by contrast, seized the opportunity to announce the arrival of that century. Bluntly he told his colleagues that they lived in a "consolidated Union" in which the states had "surrendered their equality as States, and submitted themselves to the sway of the numerical majority without qualifications or checks." He also informed them that the issues before them were moral issues; that slavery was a sin; and that Americans could not "be either true Christians or real freemen if [they] impose[d] on another a chain [they] defi[ed] all human power to fasten on [themselves]." The demands for the return of fugitive slaves smacked of the Dark Ages, and our human laws must be brought "to the standards of the law of God. . . ."

Seward, in turn, was revealing the fact that the northern mind and conscience had kept pace with the industry, the cities, the finance, and the railroads of the onrushing nineteenth century. He was making it equally clear that a realization of the dignity of a human being and a deep feeling of guilt for its violation was as marked as the material changes.

The southern demand for a more efficient fugitive-slave law which came out of the Compromise of 1850 again showed how poorly informed southern leaders were and how inadequate was their understanding of the northern mind. Nothing could have contributed more toward rendering slavery obnoxious. Nothing could have convinced the North so completely of southern inhumanity and the calloused state of the southern conscience as did this act. Yet strict northern obedience was the condition on which the southern states accepted the Compromise, and northern refusal to comply with its enforcement constituted, in the end, almost the only concrete evidence offered in support of the charge of northern aggression and of northern lack of respect for the Constitution. As one Southerner said in 1860:

> The only excuse for disunion, and the only reason that we deem the idea tolerable, is that the Constitution has been violated by the "personal liberty acts" and negro-stealing mobs of the North, and that the election of a Black Republican will show that instead of fanaticism getting cool, it is growing worse, and, therefore, the sooner the South gets clear from them the better.

"The Constitution," said another,

> affords no remedy for Southern grievances. To the Southern people the Constitution is as worthless as a piece of waste paper so far as protection to the slavery interest is concerned. The Constitution authorizes slavery; the same instrument declares that fugitives shall be returned to their masters; Congress has passed laws in accordance therewith; and the decisions of the Supreme Court affirm and maintain the mandates of the Constitution and the laws of the National Legislature.

Yet, as he said, if a master attempted to recover his servant in accord with his constitutional rights, he would be arrested, fined, and sent to prison in nine different northern states. No wonder that the Reverend J. Thornwell insisted that the original Constitution had been repealed and new terms of Union submitted for southern acceptance.

Yet, at this very moment, the Charleston *Mercury*, speaking for the only portion of the South eager for secession, was saying that the "Personal Liberty Laws" were not of the slightest consequence to the "Cotton States." "Few or none of our slaves are lost, by being carried away and protected from recapture in the Northern States." These laws only mattered "in the insult they conveyed to the South, and the evidence they offered of Northern faithlessness."

In the decade which followed the Compromise of 1850, the North as a whole moved rapidly forward into the Modern World. It was a period "when modern industrial capitalism was beginning to sink its roots deep into the American economy." Northern cities, both on the seaboard and far back in the interior, were reaching metropolitan proportions. Canals and railroads were bringing the Northeast and the Northwest closer together, and the coastal cities from Boston to Baltimore were competing for the western produce which once went largely to New Orleans. The "young industrial capitalism of textiles, iron, machinery, wood, and leather products" was no longer content to be held back by the restrictions on protection, banking, labor supply, and public works imposed by the Democratic party under southern influence. The hard, cold facts of economic and social interdependence were teaching them the value of national consolidation. The Union was an economic necessity.

Nor were the young capitalists willing to see slavery spread to the territories of the farther West. Rather, the territories should be homesteaded by free men and women and made more accessible by government aid to rivers and harbors and railroads. It took only the fictitious Uncle Tom and the unfortunate Kansas-Nebraska Bill to bring into being the sectional Republican party as the carrier of northern interests and values. These men did not clearly understand what they were doing, but they were in fact creating a political party which stood for the nationalism, the industrial capitalism, and the democratic-humanitarian impulses of the Modern World.

The southern states, meanwhile, followed their accustomed course. There were changes here as well as in the North, but they tended to strengthen old patterns, not to add new ones. More and more the Cotton Kingdom along the Gulf dominated the section. In spite of rather remarkable advances in the agriculture, industry, and transportation of the older states, "Cotton" increasingly spoke for the South. Its voice was more confident and more aggressive. Its planters had greater reasons for maintaining the status quo and more reason for fearing the attacks on slavery. The supreme confidence of its leaders in the power of Cotton to make or break the prosperity of the whole Western world provided most of the confidence with which the whole South ultimately accepted the risks in secession. It was the Cotton States' extreme demand for new guarantees for the protection of slavery in the territories which destroyed the Democratic party at Charleston.

Conservatives resented what they called "the fierce and eager instigations of the Cotton States," and border-state spokesmen insisted that the Cotton States should "bear with the few wrongs inflicted upon them, until those, who 'lose ten times as many negroes and suffer ten times as many inconveniences through the hostility of the Northern people to their institutions' " and "who stand between them and danger," should "feel it their duty and interest to act." Yet in the end those who had suffered most and would continue to suffer most, permitted those who had prospered most and suffered least to shape the section's destiny.

It was a University of Virginia professor who wrote at the time when secession was a reality:

> Indignation and alarm alternate in my breast when I think of wretched little South Carolina, like an insolent and enfeebled reactionary, plunging the whole country into strife and confusion of which others must bear the brunt. . . . And when I reflect that the mean desertion of the other Southern States compels us to make this the crisis of our destiny, whether we like it or not, I am oppressed at once with indignation and anxiety. And these feelings are aggravated by the consideration that while I think the conspirators of the cotton states deserve the condign punishment, our safety makes it necessary that we should interpose to screen them if need be. . . . They bluster and threaten, safe, as they imagine, behind the intervening tiers of quiet Commonwealths to those chivalrous feelings and sympathy they design to appeal to support them in a course abhorrent to the principles of these States and destructive to their interests.

Yet when Lincoln called for troops, the good professor was convinced that "Nothing remains now to the Christian patriot but to strike strongly for the right, humbly invoking the aid and blessing of our fathers' God."

Thus under Cotton's rule and with able assistance from the north-

ern abolitionists, from Seward, Sumner, and John Brown, the few
who from the beginning had wished to break up the Union found
the opportunity to shift the southern efforts from defense to aggression. They realized that it was not possible to dissolve the Union with
"unanimity and without division." "Men having both nerve and self-
sacrificing patriotism," said Barnwell Rhett, "must head the movement and shape its course, controlling and compelling their inferior
contemporaries." Deliberately they turned their backs on the nineteenth century. Closing their eyes to the tattered realities about them
and their minds to all the democratic-humanitarian demands of the
age in which they lived, they proclaimed the perfection of their ways
and values and their superiority over those of all the Western world.

It was the North, they said, which was deluded. What its leaders
called progress was, in fact, the real backwardness. Its celebrated cities
were breeders of crime and vice and social conflict. Its free labor system was nothing other than cruel, impersonal exploitation devoid of
all responsibility. Its chaotic social-economic system was marked by
periodic depressions, endless strife between capital and labor, and
a constant threat of revolution. Its lack of stability had destroyed all
respect for constitutional restrictions and had, at last, produced a sectional political party bent on national domination. It had produced
an eroded people who would not fight even for their own interests.

In sharp contrast to all this, they pictured the South as a wholesome rural world, orthodox in religion and untroubled by the restless
"isms" that beset the North. A peaceful world where capital and
labor were one, and where the realities of inequality between individuals and races were accepted and adjusted to the benefit of all.
The institution of slavery, instead of being a blight upon the region,
was the very foundation on which a superior civilization rested. Instead of debasing the character of the master, as charged, it produced
the highest type of leader and the man who accepted his responsi-
bilities both to his slaves and to society. Only in a slave society, where
all white men were equal, was a true democracy possible. Only where
the Negro was enslaved was he happy, productive, and free from the
worry and cares of a complex civilization for which he was ill-fitted
by nature. On the mudsills of slavery a golden age was alone possible
and all the world would one day accept the fact. The state, not the

nation, should command first allegiance. The nineteenth century was moving in the wrong direction.

It is, indeed, difficult to believe that under normal conditions any considerable number of Southerners would have accepted either the absurd notion of northern decadence or of southern perfection. But nothing, in the 1850's, could long remain normal. In the North, change crowded on the heels of change and public reaction to events, whether economic or political, no longer took form from the events themselves but from the sectional slavery controversy. There might have been some question as to the actual danger of slavery expansion from the Kansas-Nebraska Act or the Dred Scott Decision, but that did not matter. The issue was one of right and wrong. What did matter was that the "slave power" had been given the legal right to expand and that brought a firm determination to see slavery confined to its present limits and set on the road to ultimate extinction. The day for compromise with slavery had ended.

This grim northern determination, when combined with the brutal fact that the South had become a permanent political minority, its social system under moral condemnation by the whole Western world, its economic life reduced to colonial status, gave the southern extremists a new lease on life. Critics stood almost helpless before the apprehensions, the fears, the indignation, and the self-respect to which the fanatics could appeal. "All that could be done by moderate, dispassionate, patriotic, and experienced men was to go with the current, endeavoring to subdue its boiling and seething energies. . . ."

By 1860, the extreme, self-appointed spokesmen for southern rights had all but silenced their critics and sealed the southern mind against all outside opinion. They were able to split the Democratic party with demands based on their assumptions of the rightness and perfection of the slavery system. With a curious psychopathic twist at the moment of decision in the Charleston Convention, William L. Yancey of Alabama indignantly upbraided his northern colleagues for treating slavery as an evil. They should have boldly pronounced it a positive good. If they had taken the position that slavery was right by the laws of nature and of God, they would have triumphed.

To this archaic demand, George E. Pugh of Ohio gave the only answer a modern man could give and the one that would be given over and over again: "Gentlemen of the South, you mistake us—you mistake us! We will not do it."

As the campaign of 1860 developed, a once-conservative southern editor impatiently brushed aside all projects for saving the Union. They were all "feeble and fruitless" because of "the absolute impossibility of revolutionizing Northern opinion in relation to slavery."

> Without a change of heart, radical and thorough, all guarantees which might be offered are not worth the paper on which they would be enscribed. As long as slavery is looked upon by the North with abhorrence; as long as the South is regarded as a mere slave-breeding and slave-driving community; as long as false and pernicious theories are cherished respecting the inherent equality and rights of every human being, there can be no satisfactory political union between the two sections.

Northern editors were just as realistic. "We cannot tell Mr. Yancey," said one, "that we do not believe slavery wrong, for the reverse is the profound conviction of three-fourths of the whole North. . . . It would be dishonest to say that this conviction will not remain and grow stronger every day." And to promise the "complete revolution in the moral and political convictions" which the South demanded, or to promise that all opposition to slavery would cease, was like promising that "water shall run up hill and two and two shall make five."

> The strife between freedom and slavery . . . is but a fragment of the great conflict of [the] ages, the ever raging war between those things which are just, virtuous, useful, and good, and those which are hurtful and vicious and wrong.

Had not the struggle between the sections rested on such foundations as these, there might have been some way out. But as things stood, the mere election of Lincoln was "only confirmation of a purpose which the South had hoped would be abandoned by the opponents of Slavery in the North" and, which failing, drove the states of the South into "their present resistance, and their present determination to seek that safety and security out of the Union which they have been unable to obtain within it."

"In no other way," said a contemporary, "can we account for the perfect whirlwind of public feeling which swept everything before it, either utterly annihilating conservatism and nationality, or reducing to impotence the few who still ventured to make a timid appeal on behalf of the Union. . . ."

But this, after all, answers our question only in terms of the day. It ignores the fact that while there is strife and hatred "men have eyes for nothing save the fact that the enemy is the cause of all the troubles; but long, long afterwards, when all passion has been spent, the historian often sees that it was a conflict between one-half that was perhaps too wilful, and another half-right that was perhaps too proud; and behind even this he discovers that it was a terrible predicament which had the effect of putting men at cross-purposes with one another."

The historian may still question the soundness of southern leadership, but he will remember that men, whose opportunity in the Modern World was one of producing its raw cotton, did not deliberately choose to do so on plantations with Negro slavery. They only went on with what was already at hand in their hurry to prosper. And having done so without the necessity of altering to any degree their social-economic patterns, they saw no reason for changing their traditional notions of the federal character of the national government, the benefits of Negro slavery, or the superiority of a rural-agricultural way of life. The social-intellectual side of the nineteenth century had not come their way. As a result, they were sometimes confused, sometimes reduced to rationalizing, sometimes overwhelmed by guilt.

Nor should the historian give too much moral credit to northern men, upon whom had been showered all the benefits of the advancing urban-industrial age, for advocating consolidated nationalism, free labor, and democratic-humanitarian reforms. These were the social-intellectual approaches which the new age demanded of those who shared its benefits. Northern men did not in all cases deliberately choose them. They merely accepted them as part of what they were soon calling "Progress."

And so the historian, having heard both sides, begins to understand the "fundamental human predicament . . . which would have led to a serious conflict of wills even if all men had been fairly intelligent and reasonably well-intended." He may, in historical perspective, even "learn to be a little more sorry for both parties" who came to believe that they had no alternative to war. Even the war itself might lose some of its romance, cease to be simply a struggle between good men and bad men, and begin to take on its true meaning as a nation's greatest tragedy. Yet, with all this later-day understanding, no historian can ignore the fact that the southern resort to secession for the protection of slavery reduced the whole matter, for northern men of that day, to one of saving the Union and destroying slavery as an obligation to the age in which they lived.

Reconstruction: Ultraconservative Revolution

ERIC MC KITRICK

• The phrase "radical reconstruction" appears in almost every textbook in American history. It is difficult, however, to point to any permanent changes of a radical nature that resulted from Reconstruction policies. The Civil War led to the Thirteenth Amendment which abolished slavery and the Fourteenth which granted citizenship to anyone born or naturalized in the United States and which required states to proceed with "due process of law" (however ambiguous that may be) before depriving any citizen of life, liberty, or property. These constitutional amendments passed through Congress before Reconstruction in the South began. Beginning in 1867 military forces occupied the southern states and influenced the region's politics for almost a decade. But in crucial areas such as social mobility, education, and occupational opportunities, little was done to help the former slave. No major political or military figures of the Confederacy suffered anything more than temporary imprisonment and suspension of political rights for a few years. The structure of southern society remained relatively intact and the descendants of the pre-Civil War leaders emerged as the key personages in the post-Reconstruction South. For all of these reasons, as well as others discussed below, Eric McKitrick argues that Reconstruction was not radical but "ultraconservative." His analysis also provides insights into some of the more troubling questions of our own era.

From *The Comparative Approach to American History*, edited by C. Vann Woodward. Copyright © 1968 by C. Vann Woodward. Reprinted by permission of Basic Books, Inc., Publishers, New York.

It had been understood for some time that the American Civil War was a revolution. But more than a hundred years have had to pass before Americans can finally begin to understand what sort of revolution it actually was. Not so many years ago our historians were still arguing that the Civil War—"the Second American Revolution," as the late Charles Beard called it—represented the final victory of Northern capitalism in its relentless aggressions against the agrarian economy of the South, and that slavery was in no true sense the central issue. Such a point of view was first encouraged by Marx and Engels, who observed the war and followed its course with great interest, and arguments based on some version of that same viewpoint have not entirely disappeared from the discussions of historians even today. Other writers in turn have argued that the Civil War should not be considered as a Marxian revolution of North against South, but rather as a revolution of the South against the United States—that slavery *was* indeed the central issue, and that in order to preserve slavery the Southern states were willing to undertake a war of liberation. The true revolutionary act, then, was the South's effort to achieve separation from the Federal Union. And yet by viewing the Reconstruction that followed the Civil War, and by considering it and the war together as parts of the same process, we begin to see that perhaps the North was, in a larger sense, the revolutionary aggressor after all. Moreover, by connecting these events with the events of today as part of an even larger pattern, we may see at last what sort of revolution it really was. We may see that its deepest, most pressing, most fundamental issue was, and still is, the proper place of the American Negro in American life. And we may even wonder, as we consider the experience of Reconstruction, whether the American political and constitutional structure itself provides a truly adequate framework within which the revolution may be brought to a satisfactory as well as peaceful close.

It has been very difficult for historians or anyone else to view all this as a single revolutionary cycle. One reason is that the cycle has been so long: it began at least a generation before the Civil War and has not yet ended. But the more important reason is that its central problem—the Negro's place in American life—was one which Americans were never willing to confront directly, even at the most critical phases of the revolution, those of the Civil War and Reconstruction.

This confusion, this ambiguity, this reluctance to face the implications of a problem of such magnitude, have had curious effects on Americans' very habits of historical thought. Despite the enormous and persistent interest in the Civil War, and despite the lesser but still considerable interest in Reconstruction, the latter period has become intellectually encapsulated. It has been isolated within the national consciousness and the national memory in a very unusual way, considering the things that a revolution does to a nation's life. With regard to the objectives of the Reconstruction, even of the Civil War, the quality of our writing, our thought, and our public discourse has been very diffuse and has shown a remarkable lack of precision. Nevertheless, the demands of the 1960's have made it clear that the revolution is not yet finished, that it has not gone nearly far enough, and that the original character of the revolution must be considered all over again.

The problem, indeed, was systematically quarantined from the very first, even while society was beginning to concede its urgency. In a way this is understandable. In almost every ordinary sense the United States on the eve of the Civil War was politically, socially, and economically one of the most stable countries in the world. A political and constitutional system had been established which was acceptable to virtually the entire population. It was characterized by universal white manhood suffrage and a level of citizen participation not seen since the days of the Greek republics. Its electoral practices may have included strong elements of demagoguery and vulgar carnival appeal, but the result was a system of party government which was in many respects the most sophisticated in the world. And whereas most European countries at mid-century were permeated with the ferment of social revolution, the United States was perhaps the one nation in the Western world where the overwhelming bulk of the population was profoundly committed to laissez-faire capitalism. It had no tory class, no tory socialism, no aristocracy with traditions of noblesse oblige or a sense of responsibility for checking the excesses of laissez faire. American society, as Tocqueville had discovered a generation earlier, had become intensely egalitarian and intensely committed to the ideal of equal opportunity and careers open to talent. It would be difficult for most Europeans to understand that those values normally regarded elsewhere as "bourgeois" were in 1860 the values of the American farmer, the American workingman, and the American enterpreneur.

All of these values were embodied in the career and person of Abraham Lincoln, who was to be the leader of the "revolutionary" party of 1860. Lincoln, rising from the poorest possible origins, largely self-educated, a leader in politics while still a young man, becoming a successful railroad lawyer, and emerging from state politics in Ilinois to become the Republican nominee for the Presidency, insisted again and again that there was no real gulf between capital and labor. "There is no permanent class of hired laborers amongst us," he announced in one of several speeches he made on this subject in 1859. "Twenty-five years ago, I was a hired laborer. The hired laborer of yesterday, labors on his own account today; and will hire others to labor for him to-morrow. Advancement—improvement in condition— is the order of things in a society of equals." Probably few men of any class who heard these words would have thought of doubting their essential truth. For most Americans living in the North, this highly satisfactory state of affairs had come to be directly connected with the continued stability of the Federal Union. The one great flaw in it, as Lincoln reminded his audiences in each of these speeches, was the continued existence of a very rigid system of chattel slavery.

Americans had inevitably been brought to confront this problem. But they did so reluctantly, despite the steady growth of antislavery feeling which had already begun to force itself into national politics by the 1840's. This feeling could only be admitted into the realm of political discourse and contention by placing all stress upon the Union and virtually none upon the Negro, in order to maintain some sort of unity even in the North. It was done not by a direct assault upon slavery, but through the formula of "Free Soil": not by challenging slavery where it was, but by declaring that it should not be carried into new places where it did not yet exist. In short, men did face the issue, but they deliberately avoided facing it directly as long as they possibly could.

Even after the war broke out, they continued to avoid it. In order to prevent the alienation of a sizable portion of the Northern people, to say nothing of the border states which had not seceded, the administration felt it necessary to declare that its sole purpose in waging war was to restore the Federal Union. Lincoln announced this on many occasions in the most solemn tones. "I would save the Union," he insisted; "I would save it the shortest way under the Constitution. The sooner the national authority can be restored, the nearer the Union will be 'the Union as it was.' . . . My paramount object in this struggle is to save the Union, and is *not* either to save or to destroy slavery." And yet the man to whom this was written—Horace Greeley, editor of the influential New York *Tribune*—himself represented a growing sector of public opinion which was insisting that emancipation should be made one of the objects of the war. It had already become obvious to Lincoln by the summer of 1862 that without the support of this sector the continued vigor of the war effort might itself be undermined; and although he had told Greeley, "If I could save the Union without freeing any slave, I would do it," he also conceded that if he "could do it by freeing all the slaves," he would do that. But if he conceded this much, he was hardly prepared to go the whole way, because he too understood public opinion, probably better than Greeley. The Emancipation Proclamation (which, according to one of our historians, "had all the moral grandeur of a bill of lading") was presented not as a statement of high purpose but as a measure of military necessity.

It was the same with regard to the use of Negro troops in the Union Army. Two objectives might be served by accepting Negro enlistments. One of them directly concerned the Negro himself: "Once let the black man get upon his person the brass letters, U.S.," as the Negro abolitionist Frederick Douglass expressed it, ". . . and there is no power on earth which can deny that he has earned the right to citizenship in the United States." The other was that Negro soldiers might augment the declining strength of the army and thus assist in suppressing the rebellion. Of the two objectives, the Northern public would accept only the second. Even this could occur only after the war was well under way, and after many discouraging military reverses. Few concessions were made to the Negro's representing any more than a matter of military policy. Negro regiments could have no Negro officers, and the United States Congress refused to grant them equal pay with white troops until the war was nearly over. The Negro's proper role, even in the society of wartime, could not be considered on its own terms but only in the interest of some other objective. Even the President, despite his "oft-expressed personal wish that all men everywhere could be free," could still think of no more satisfactory way of dealing with slaves who had been freed than to encourage them to leave the country. His "first impulse," he had stated in 1854, "would be to free all the slaves and send them to Liberia"; eight years later, on the very eve of emancipation, he was earnestly urging a committee of Negro leaders to colonize themselves and their families in Central America, as the best example that could be offered to American Negroes everywhere.

II

Once the war was over, the problem of dealing both with the Negro and with the readmission of Southern states to the Federal Union dominated all else. But all emphasis was placed upon the latter. And again, the first instinct was to change as little as possible. By constitutional amendment the Negro had been given his freedom, but few steps were taken to adjust him to his new status. At the same time elaborate efforts were made by the administration of Lincoln's successor, Andrew Johnson, to re-establish state governments in the South which would be more or less identical with those in existence before the war. Certain things were rejected almost out of hand. There was to be no redistribution of land, either with or without compensation. There was no insistence that Negroes be accorded rights of citizenship. Federal responsibility for education and welfare was regarded as being only of the most temporary and limited kind. Legislation to expand even the minimal services of this sort that did exist— those performed by the wartime Freedmen's Bureau—was opposed by the President, and there were not enough votes in the national Congress to enact it over his veto. It is certainly true that the President's position on these questions lagged behind that of the Republican majority in Congress, and perhaps even somewhat behind the center position in public opinion. But the differences, in 1865 and 1866, were hardly more than differences in degree.

The revolution was destined to go considerably further than anything Andrew Johnson had in mind. But its conservative nature would still be such, even at its height, as to make it hardly comparable to any other revolutionary or counterrevolutionary movement known to modern Western history. Not one political prisoner, for example, was ever put to death. The political head of the rebellion was kept in prison for two years and then set free, while the rebellion's military chief was never molested at all. The President of the United States spent much of his time during the first year of peace over matters of amnesty and pardon; and a few years later, while Congressional Reconstruction was still in full force, an act of general amnesty in effect removed that problem from further contention altogether. The government of Soviet Russia was executing enemies of the Revolution years after the Revolution itself was over. Even in England, whose revolution was one of the earliest and mildest, the revolutionary party felt it expedient to execute the head of the state, after having done away with his two chief advisors, and to massacre priests, women, and children in Ireland. With the Restoration, only the genial disposition of the king himself prevented a blood bath of vengeance and limited the number of executions to a dozen regicides.

The political, constitutional, legal, and administrative changes effected in the United States through the Civil War and Reconstruction were almost invisible compared with those that remained in France from the French Revolution, even after the restoration of the Bourbon monarchy. There, the provincial boundaries of the Old Regime were eliminated forever (in the America of 1865 and 1866, the very thought of such a thing made men turn pale with consternation); while the new geographical boundaries were designed in such a way that the resulting "departments" could be uniformly administered through the central government in Paris. (In the American South, even today, mere "interference" by the central government is the issue most likely to unite the entire population.) The most sweeping changes in property, class, fiscal, and jurisdictional relationships throughout French society, effected by the Revolution and codified by Bonaparte, were never reversed despite all efforts by the Bourbons to turn back the clock. The American "Bourbons," as the South's post-Reconstruction leaders were called, hardly needed to turn back the clock at all. No changes on this scale had been effected in the first place. As for the emancipated slaves, far less was done for them by the United States government in the way of land distribution and social planning than was done during that very same period for the emancipated serfs of autocratic imperial Russia.

By 1867 the extraordinary refusal of President Andrew Johnson to

cooperate with Northern leadership on any of the problems of readjustment, plus the determination of the South to resist even the
minimal implications of change, had brought the North—still
reluctantly—to see the need for stronger measures. The result was
called "Radical Reconstruction." These measures, designed to protect
Negroes and those Southern whites who had supported the Union,
represented the high point of revolutionary action. The military occupation, followed by the enfranchisement of the entire Negro male
population, the temporary disqualification of former Confederate
leaders from suffrage and officeholding, and the establishment and
support of state governments heavily dependent upon Negro votes
and operated by pro-Union whites and Negroes constituted the
closest thing to a revolutionary situation that was reached.

This situation, which began deteriorating almost at once, lasted
no more than a few years. By 1877 all of the so-called "Radical" state
governments had been expelled, mostly through the force of local
pressure. Two general criticisms of this experiment may be made, not
counting the traditional one that the Southern white people had been
forced for a time to accept regimes which they did not want. One
is that this relatively radical political program was not accompanied
by anything systematic in the way of social and economic welfare.
Much of what was accomplished in matters of education, for example,
had to be undertaken through private efforts by Northern philan-
thropic groups, and in the face of enormous local resistance. There
was no confiscation of estates, and no systematic effort to aid the
freedmen in acquiring holdings of their own. Thus it might be said
that the true priorities were reversed: that the Negro was given the
vote before he had either the education or the economic power that
would enable him to make effective use of it. The other criticism
is that, even if it were granted that political rights ought to have
come first after all, the federal government was still unprepared to
undertake the massive commitment of long-term supervision, combined with continuing force, that would have been needed to preserve
those rights.

Thus in the face of corruption, inefficiency, and chronic local aggression and unrest, the federal government gradually withdrew its
support and allowed the white community in each state to re-establish

full control. By 1877 the political, social, and economic systems of the South had become remarkably similar to what they had been in 1860, except that now the Negro was a landless laborer rather than a legally bound slave. A final stage of reaction remained. In the general effort to reconstitute the structure which had been disrupted by the Civil War and Reconstruction, even the Negro's small political gains—to say nothing of the minimal social rights he had acquired, in no way commensurate with the total effort and sacrifices implied in that war—were systematically removed. One by one, and with no interference whatever, the Southern states now began by law to impose systems of social segregation and disfranchisement which set the Negro entirely outside the mainstream of Southern civic life. By 1900 the process was virtually complete.

III

Without a clear center of gravity, historical discussion of this entire problem has had a somewhat erratic character. For the most part, it has been considered well within the context of the American constitutional system, and with very cautious assumptions, quite orthodox and traditional, as to where the boundaries of that system are located. One line of thought, probably more persistent than any other, regards the whole episode of Reconstruction with the most profound distaste, because it prolonged into peacetime the internal conflicts and alienations which had driven the American people into fratricidal war. The Civil War and Reconstruction thus represented a breach that must above all be healed, smoothed over, reknit. Perhaps the definitive statement of this position was made by Paul Buck in his *Road to Reunion, 1865–1900*. Yet it may also be significant that the terminal date of Professor Buck's study coincides with that very point in time at which the Negro's own exclusion from American society had been made all but complete.

My own study of Andrew Johnson's role in Reconstruction, published seven years ago, also assumes reunion to be a primary value, without questioning the limits of the system as it then existed. I argued, perhaps somewhat conservatively, that within those limits, and without violating the basic assumptions and values of the most enlightened men of the time, far more might have been done toward solving the problems of Reconstruction, as well as of reunion, than was in fact done. And yet these assumptions might themselves be questioned. An English historian of great perception and intelligence, William R. Brock, has recently looked at the subject of Reconstruction through the eyes of an outsider. He concludes that the very system of federalism, as established by the Constitution and construed by two generations of pre-Civil War Americans, was simply not adequate for the containment of a problem of such dimensions and magnitude.

As the problem confronts us all over again in the 1960's, we might well consider the bare possibility, at least, of Brock's being right. It could be argued that the decision to commit federal power to Reconstruction would not have been taken at all but for the abnormal stimulus of a crisis between the executive and legislative branches of the federal government. Then, as the will to maintain that commitment began to wane, there remained to the states—thanks to the federal "balance"—all the power they needed to expel with relative ease those features of Reconstruction they found not to their liking. By the turn of the century the states, using the authority of their state governments to render federal law inoperative, could place restrictions on the political and social rights of Negroes which the judicial branch of the federal government could overlook only by allowing the law to be construed in a highly strained and dubious way. These restrictions—virtual disfranchisement and complete social segregation— remained until World War II almost wholly unchallenged. As late as 1964 the Assistant Attorney General in charge of civil rights, Burke Marshall, was not optimistic about the future of federal law enforcement. At that time Mr. Marshall devoted two public lectures at a major university to the inherent restrictions imposed by the very structure of the federal system. Even the guarantee of voting rights, despite a series of federal laws beginning in 1957 which simply attempted to enforce the Fifteenth Amendment, had been for practical purposes frustrated in innumerable Southern communities.

Thus in view of what is minimally indispensable to complete the revolution begun with emancipation and Reconstruction, the restrictions of the federal structure do indeed seem formidable. The minimum obligations go well beyond political rights. They include full employment and whatever is necessary to guarantee it: special programs of training, the full opening of union membership, and the elimination of job discrimination. They include massive support for education, recognizing that the need for special compensatory instruction enormously complicates a problem complex enough already. They include a vast expansion of municipal recreation facilities, and automatic government responsibility in all cases of major social disturbance. They include adequate housing, which means not simply a great deal more low-cost public housing but open access to all housing, even to the point of public guarantees of property values. Whatever the present restrictions of the federal structure, it seems imperative that any real movement toward realizing these aims requires a national government with the power to act.

And yet this is hardly as utopian as may now appear, nor need one be so quick to assume that the governmental structure of federalism is the truly critical factor. History itself shows us otherwise. It is rather a question of the community's will to use what powers its federal government already has. Mr. Marshall's pessimism in 1964 over Negro voter registration, for example, was rendered to a considerable extent out of date after two more years of focused federal legislation and effort, and resistance to Negro registration is no longer the major issue it was then. Or, to go back a full century: although there was not the remotest constitutional precedent for the Reconstruction legislation of 1867, the majority found a constitutional sanction for it anyway, strained though it may have been, in the obligation of Congress to guarantee to each state a republican form of government. During the New Deal period of the 1930's, federal intervention in state affairs went beyond anything most men would have thought possible a few years before. And this was nothing to the vast scope which federal power allowed itself for the purposes of fighting World War II. Controlling and directing the entire national economy, and in effect regulating the lives of millions of people, both military and civilian, the federal government impinged itself on the rights of the citizenry to a degree vastly exceeding anything that would be required to fulfill every demand of the Negro revolution. The difference was that in its objectives the government had the overwhelming support of the entire society.

It is a matter not so much of the government's defining its powers as the community's defining its needs. Even the "revolutionary" terminology I have been using up to now may be more confusing than enlightening. The problem of the Negro's place in American life was one which, despite the upheavals of emancipation and Reconstruction, had by 1900 been solved in a way that a majority of Americans found satisfactory. A majority today is finding that same "solution" not only unsatisfactory but intolerable. Times have changed, and it is not simply the moral weather that has changed; the very conditions of community life have changed.

The "revolution," if we wish to go on calling it that, has shifted to the Northern cities, and thinking on federal civil rights policy has shifted from voting rights to matters of much broader social and economic significance. The problem of race relations is now of such a nature that it can no longer be encapsulated as it could be in post-Reconstruction times. Moreover, the problem is inexorable; its dynamic element is an increasing concentration of Negroes in urban areas, and the lives of a majority of Americans are coming to be tied in more and more ways to the condition of the Negro community. Whatever the immediate vicissitudes of the question—the "backlash" vote in the 1966 elections, the continued preference of Southern communities for segregationist candidates, the failure of the 1966 civil rights bill—the problem will not go away. It is there, and there it remains; no one living in an American city can escape it.

The situation contains elements today which it did not have in Reconstruction, and broadening the battleground to include the Northern cities has perhaps for the first time provided a base upon which the problem can be—as indeed it must be—truly nationalized. In such a setting there is no longer any way to avoid dealing with the Negro as a functioning part of the community's economic, social, and political life. It is here that the pressure and energy needed to sustain a high level of federal concern are most likely to be generated, and as a more and more substantial portion of the decision-making community accustoms itself to acting systematically and conceiving policy in massive terms, the sooner a base will be built upon which permanent national standards may be formed.

The complexities of the federal system have often functioned in an inhibitive way, and pockets of regional resistance have traditionally operated to undermine the national will. And yet whenever standards of national necessity have had majority support, and where majority will has been present for insisting upon such standards, the abstract rigidities of the federal system have had a way of becoming surprisingly fluid. History does provide us tests for this. They are, as I have said, such as may be found in the depression years of the 1930's, in World War II, in the Civil War, and even—though in a form we can now see as much too temporary—in Reconstruction.